cheesecake

cheesecake

60 classic and original recipes for heavenly desserts

Hannah Miles

photography by Steve Painter

LONDON • NEW YORK

To Gregg Wallace and John Torode, Masterchef Judges
extraordinaire and lovers of a good buttery biscuit base!

DESIGN, PHOTOGRAPHY AND PROP STYLING Steve Painter
EDITOR Rebecca Woods
HEAD OF PRODUCTION Patricia Harrington
ART DIRECTOR Leslie Harrington
EDITORIAL DIRECTOR Julia Charles

FOOD STYLIST Lucy McKelvie
FOOD STYLIST'S ASSISTANT Ellie Jarvis
ILLUSTRATIONS Tinckelly Illustration
INDEXER Hilary Bird

First published in 2013 by
Ryland Peters & Small
20–21 Jockey's Fields
London WC1R 4BW
and
519 Broadway, 5th Floor
New York, NY 10012

www.rylandpeters.com
10 9 8 7 6 5 4 3 2 1

Text © Hannah Miles 2013
Design, illustrations and photographs © Ryland Peters & Small 2013

Printed in China

ISBN: 978-1-84975-352-4

A CIP record for this book is available from the British Library.
US Library of Congress CIP data has been applied for.

NOTES
• All spoon measurements are level unless otherwise specified.
• All eggs are large (UK) or extra large (US), unless otherwise specified.
Uncooked or partially cooked eggs should not be served to the very old, frail,
young children, pregnant women or those with compromised immune systems.
• When using cling film/plastic wrap in the oven, make sure you use a brand
which is heatproof and suitable for this purpose.
• Ovens should be preheated to the specified temperatures. We recommend
using an oven thermometer. If using a fan-assisted oven, adjust temperatures
according to the manufacturer's instructions.

contents

introduction

Cheesecake, *käsekuchen*, *tarta de queso*, *gâteau au fromage* – however you know this delicious dessert, one thing is certain, the humble cheesecake has universal appeal. Almost every country in the world has its own cheesecake tradition and they are one of the world's oldest desserts, with records dating cheesecakes back even as far as 200 BC. Quite frankly, I don't know anyone who doesn't love a slice of a good cheesecake! This book contains a wide variety of flavours and styles of cheesecake with something for every taste. For those who like rich indulgent cheesecakes, why not try the *Rocky Road Cheesecake* on page 61 or the *Peanut Brittle Cheesecake* on page 58, both decorated with indulgent candy toppings. For the more flavour adventurous of you, the *Salty Honey Cheesecake* on page 84 or the *Toasted Marshmallow Cheesecake Pie* on page 118, are both quirky but utterly delicious! For those who like a good old-fashioned cheesecake, then the Classic Cheesecake chapter is for you with recipes for traditional baked *Simply Vanilla Cheesecake*, *New York Cheesecake* and even the classic 1970s retro throwback – *Fruits of the Forest Cheesecake*. For an extravagant dessert, why not serve the *Profiterole Cheesecake* on page 96, inspired by the classic French *croquembouche* and complete with a crown of spun sugar, or turn to page 83 for the *Hibiscus, Raspberry and Pomegranate Cheesecake* decorated spectacularly with hibiscus flowers and caramel sugar swirls. Whatever your favourite flavour, there is a delicious cheesecake recipe in this book for you.

TYPES OF CHEESECAKE

There are three main types of cheesecake. The classic cheesecake is a **baked** cheesecake, baked at a low temperature in the oven and set with eggs. The resulting dessert is rich and dense and you need only serve small slices for each portion. The popular *New York Cheesecake* (now eaten all over the world), such as the recipe on page 19 is the perfect example of a baked cheesecake.

Gelatine cheesecakes are the second type of cheesecake and are very different from baked cheesecakes – they are light and airy and don't require any cooking. People can often be intimidated by gelatine but these concerns are misplaced as it is really very easy to use. Using gelatine combined with cream cheese and cream gives a delicate cheesecake with a creamy consistency, without being overly heavy – making it possible to eat a much larger portion! My favourite recipe in this book – the *Plum Crumble Cheesecake* on page 49 – is a gelatine cheesecake and I could eat slice after slice!

The third type of cheesecake – a **refrigerator** cheesecake – is by far the easiest, simply whisking together soft cheese and crème fraîche with flavouring and leaving to set in the refrigerator overnight. These cheesecakes are not as light as gelatine cheesecakes but are particularly delicious flavoured with citrus, for example the *Blueberry and Lemon Cheesecake* on page 15. For a Christmassy cheesecake, why not try the *Peppermint Bark Cheesecake* on page 73?

Traditionally all of the above cheesecakes have a crumb base made with crushed biscuits/cookies and melted butter. The most common biscuit/cookie used is the humble digestive biscuit or graham cracker but as you will see from the recipes in this book, it is possible to use almost any type of biscuit or cookie – choc chip hazelnut, Oreos, custard creams or chocolate oat cookies all work well and the *Jelly and Custard Cheesecake* base on page 114 is even made with pink wafers! It is possible, however, to make cheesecakes without a biscuit/cookie base, which is particularly good for those who can't eat gluten. To replace the crunch of the biscuit/cookie crumbs, you can substitute a layer of toasted nuts, such as in the *Crunchy Almond Cheesecake* on page 99. Some of the cheesecakes in this book have been made with a cake base, which gives an altogether softer consistency but is no less delicious. Examples of these are the *Japanese Cherry Blossom Cheesecake* on page 134, which has a delicate green tea-flavoured sponge base and the *Strawberry and Cream Cheesecake* on page 54, which has a gluten-free almond sponge base. Once you have got the hang of the basic cheesecake recipes, you can experiment with different bases of your choosing.

CLASSIC CHEESECAKE INGREDIENTS

The ingredients required to make cheesecake are very simple and are readily available. Unsurprisingly, every cheesecake is made with cheese but there are many different varieties you can use.

Cream cheese is the most common cheese used in cheesecakes and is available in all supermarkets. It is important that you bring cream cheese to room temperature before using so that it is easier to mix and doesn't form lumps in the cheesecake batter.

Mascarpone cheese is a light and creamy cheese originating from Italy. It is slightly sweeter than cream cheese and is commonly used in the Italian dessert, tiramisù. It is perfect in refrigerator cheesecakes, combined with crème fraîche.

Ricotta is not technically a cheese as it is produced from whey, a byproduct of cheese making. It has a more solid texture than cream cheese and needs to be beaten well to make it smooth enough to use in cheesecake recipes. It is often used in Italian recipes and appears in many of the cheesecake recipes in this book.

Quark is a curd cheese and is very popular in Germany, although it is readily available in supermarkets in the UK and some in the USA (if you can't find it, you could substitute farmer cheese). It has a creamy consistency (quite similar to fromage frais) and slightly sour flavour, which is very refreshing in cheesecakes.

Twaróg is a Polish cheese that is similar to cottage cheese and is used to make the popular Polish cheesecake *sernik*. It comes in both natural and low-fat varieties and is available in good supermarkets and in Polish delicatessens. It has a firm consistency and needs to be passed through a fine mesh sieve/strainer or processed in a food processor before using otherwise your cheesecake will have a grainy texture.

Eggs are an essential component of baked cheesecakes as they enable the cheesecake to set. Always use the best quality eggs you can afford as they make a difference to the flavour and colour of a cheesecake. All eggs in the recipes in this book are large (UK) or extra large (US).

Gelatine – like many people, I used to face using gelatine with fear and trepidation. Such fear is unfounded as gelatine is easy to use and is a perfect setting agent for non baked cheesecakes. The recipes in this book are made with sheets of leaf gelatine, easily available in supermarkets, which are soaked in water to soften them, then squeezed out before being dissolved in a warm liquid. It is important that the liquid is only warm and not hotter as putting gelatine into boiling liquid will affect the setting properties. If you want to substitute powdered gelatine in any of the recipes in this book then, generally, 4 sheets of leaf gelatine equate to 25 g/1 oz. of powdered gelatine. This will depend on the bloom properties of the gelatine so always check the packet of your gelatine powder as they will have conversion rates on them. There is no need to soak the powdered gelatine before using, simply sprinkle it over the warm liquid in the recipe and whisk in thoroughly.

Sweeteners – all dessert cheesecakes need to be sweetened. The recipes in this book use white, brown and muscovado sugars, maple, corn and golden syrups, condensed milk, honey and icing/confectioners' sugar as sweeteners. The level of sweetness in a cheesecake is very much a matter of personal taste, so always add the sweetener gradually and taste for sweetness before adding the remainder if you do not like overly sweet desserts.

MAKING LOWER FAT CHEESECAKES

I am not going to deny it – classic cheesecakes are quite calorie laden. Purists may argue that using lower fat substitutes don't give as good a result, but whilst that might have some truth, it is perfectly possible to substitute reduced fat cream cheese, double/heavy cream, ricotta and mascarpone for their full fat counterparts in these recipes if you prefer. You can also reduce the sugar content or use a sugar substitute if you wish. The only thing I would avoid is replacing the butter in the biscuit/cookie crumb base with low-fat spreads as they simply don't taste nearly as nice. Instead, cut out the butter altogether by replacing the biscuit/cookie base with a layer of toasted nuts, which won't require any butter other than for lightly greasing the pan.

BASIC EQUIPMENT

Very little equipment is needed for making a cheese-cake. You will need an electric mixer, balloon whisk or stand mixer for whisking together the cheesecake mixture to ensure there are no lumps and a blender or rolling pin to create the biscuit/cookie crumbs for the base. You also need a good quality springform cake pan. These have a loose base and removable sides, which make it easier to remove the cheesecake from the pan and transfer to a serving plate. You must ensure that your cheesecake pan is tightly fitting otherwise the cheesecake mixture may leak or water may seep into the cheesecake if you are baking it in a waterbath. To test whether the pan seals properly, pour some water into the pan before greasing to check that it does not leak. Wrapping the the pan in a layer of cling film/plastic wrap will also prevent water getting into the pan (see Cooking Baked Cheesecakes).

Lining the cheesecake pan
Because of the fairly fragile nature of cheesecakes, particularly gelatine cheesecakes, removing them from the pan can be a tricky business. Always use a springform pan for best results and slide a knife around the edge of the cheesecake before releasing the sides of the base. Line the base of the pan with non-stick baking paper so that you can easily lift the cheesecake from the base. When you do so, make sure that your serving plate is very close at hand so that you don't have to move the cheesecake too far. Sliding a round-bladed knife under the cheesecake base will free it from the bottom of the cake pan.

COOKING BAKED CHEESECAKES

One essential element when baking cheesecakes is a consistent temperature, as changes in temperature can cause a cheesecake to crack (see Troubleshooting). One of the best ways to avoid this is to cook the cheesecake in a waterbath to ensure that the whole of the cheesecake is cooked at an even temperature. To create the waterbath you need a deep roasting pan which is larger than the size of your cheesecake pan. Wrap the outside of the cheesecake pan with a good layer of heatproof cling film/plastic wrap to prevent any water leaking into the cheesecake. If the pan does leak, it will make the base of the cheesecake soggy, which is definitely something to be avoided. Prepare the cheesecake in the wrapped pan, then place into the roasting pan and fill the roasting pan with water so that water comes about half way up the side of your cheesecake pan. Bake in the oven until the cheesecake is set with a slight wobble in the centre.

TROUBLESHOOTING

Cheesecakes are easy to make and do not often go wrong, although there are a few common issues that can arise:

Cheesecake is not properly set

If the recipe is a gelatine cheesecake, you need to make sure that you measure the ingredients very carefully as the gelatine will only set a certain quantity of liquid. Use a measuring jug or cups to measure all liquids accurately. It is also worth making sure you check the packet of any gelatine that has been sitting in the kitchen cupboard for a while as if it is past its 'use by' date this may affect its setting properties.

If a baked cheesecake has not set, it has not been cooked for long enough. The length of time you need to bake the cheesecake will depend on the actual temperature in your oven as not all ovens cook at the same temperature. (You may find it worthwhile investing in an oven thermometer.) It is best to judge whether a cheesecake is cooked by eye. It needs to be set almost completely but should still have a slight wobble in the centre. The cheesecake will continue to cook slightly from the heat of the pan as it cools, so will be perfectly set by the time it is cold. If the whole cheesecake wobbles, it has not been cooked for long enough. Return it to the oven and bake a little longer before checking again.

Cheesecake cracks on top

Cheesecakes can crack on top if they are baked at too high a temperature or if they undergo a rapid change in temperature. It is best to cook cheesecake for a long time at a low oven temperature, rather than at a high heat. When the cheesecake is cooked you can turn off the heat and leave the cheesecake to cool in the oven as the gradual decrease in temperature is ideal for cooling the cheesecake and helps prevent cracking. Cheesecakes are also less likely to crack if, before cooling, you slide a round-bladed knife around the edge of the sides of the pan. As the cheesecake cools it will shrink and if it is stuck to the sides of the pan this can cause cracking. However cracking does not affect the taste of the cheesecake and any cracks can easily be disguised under a cheesecake topping.

Lumpy cheesecake batter

As mentioned above, it is important to bring cream cheese to room temperature before using to prevent lumps. Always whisk the ingredients together well. If your mixture is still lumpy, strain it through a sieve/strainer, then press through any lumps with the back of a spoon and return to the mixture.

STORING AND FREEZING CHEESECAKES

Cheesecakes store well and I actually find they are best eaten a day or so after they have been made as the flavours have time to develop. It is important that you properly chill your cheesecakes before serving them as lukewarm cheesecakes are not very nice at all. All the cheesecakes in this book should be stored in the refrigerator (in a sealed container or wrapped with cling film/plastic wrap) as they contain dairy products, and will keep for up to a week, although cheesecakes topped with fresh cream or fresh fruit toppings really need to be eaten within 2–3 days.

Some cheesecakes can be frozen so make the ideal standby or prepare-ahead dessert. Gelatine does not freeze well so I do not recommend freezing any of the recipes in this book that contain gelatine. However both baked and refrigerator cheesecakes (which do not contain gelatine) freeze well. You should make the cheesecake following the recipe but do not decorate it. Once the cheesecake has cooled completely and is set, remove from the pan and transfer it to a plate or baking sheet. Wrap the cheesecake carefully in several layers of cling film/plastic wrap and transfer to the freezer. Once the cheesecake has frozen, you can remove the plate or baking sheet, rewrap the cheesecake and return to the freezer. Store in the freezer in this way for up to a month for best results. Alternatively, you can cut a baked cheesecake into slices and freeze as individual portions if you prefer. Always freeze the cheesecake without its topping. To defrost, place the cheesecake on a plate in the refrigerator and leave to defrost overnight, then prepare any cheesecake topping following the steps in the recipe.

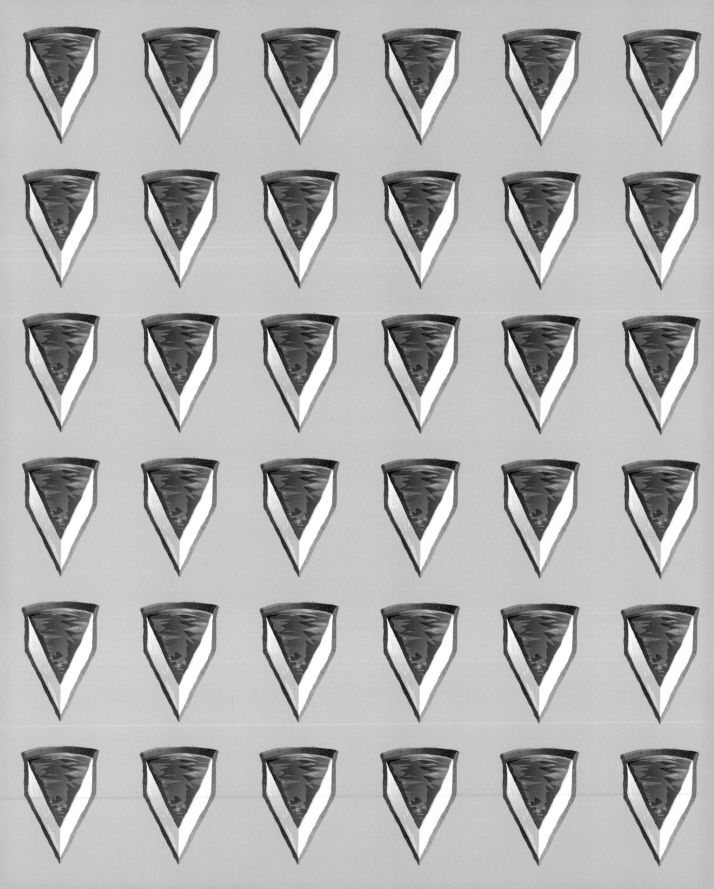

classic cheesecakes

simply vanilla cheesecake

This cheesecake is simple but is always popular with my friends and family – no frills, no fuss, just a good old fashioned vanilla. It is delicious served with fresh berries of your choice and a little pouring cream.

FOR THE CRUMB CASE

300 g/10½ oz. digestive biscuits/graham crackers

150 g/1¼ sticks butter, melted

FOR THE FILLING

600 ml/2½ cups crème fraîche

750 g/3⅓ cups cream cheese

4 eggs

400 g/1¾ cups condensed milk

2 tablespoons plain/all-purpose flour, sifted

1 vanilla pod/bean

TO SERVE

fresh berries of your choice

pouring cream

a 26-cm/10-inch round springform cake pan, greased and lined

SERVES 12

Preheat the oven to 170°C (325°F) Gas 3.

To make the crumb case, crush the biscuits/graham crackers to fine crumbs in a food processor or place in a clean plastic bag and bash with a rolling pin. Transfer the crumbs to a mixing bowl and stir in the melted butter. Press the buttery crumbs into the base and sides of the prepared cake pan firmly using the back of a spoon. You need the crumbs to come up about 3–4 cm/1½ inches high on the side of the pan so that they make a case for the filling. Wrap the outside of the pan in cling film/plastic wrap and place in a roasting pan half full with water, ensuring that the water is not so high as to spill out. Set aside.

For the filling, whisk together the crème fraîche, cream cheese, eggs, condensed milk and flour. Using a sharp knife split the vanilla pod/bean in half, scrape out the seeds from both halves and add to the cheesecake mixture, discarding the pod/bean (see tip below). Whisk until the seeds are evenly distributed, then pour the mixture into the crumb case. Transfer the cheesecake, in its waterbath, to the oven and bake for 1–1¼ hours until golden brown on top and still with a slight wobble in the centre. Remove the cheesecake from the waterbath and slide a knife around the edge of the pan to release the cheesecake and prevent it from cracking. Leave to cool, then transfer to the refrigerator to chill for at least 3 hours or preferably overnight. Serve with berries and pouring cream.

Tip: You can store the left over vanilla pod/bean in a jar of sugar to make vanilla sugar for baking.

blueberry and lemon cheesecake

In my first round on BBC's Masterchef I made this cheesecake and served it to John and Gregg, the judges. They liked it a lot – so much so that Gregg picked up the cheesecake and pressed it into his face. Filming had to stop whilst they washed Gregg's shirt and cleared away any evidence of blueberry juice. I think I knew then that I stood a good chance of going through to the next round!

FOR THE TOPPING

350 g/2½–3 cups blueberries

freshly squeezed juice of 2 lemons

100 g/½ cup caster/white sugar

FOR THE CRUMB BASE

200 g/7 oz. digestive biscuits/
graham crackers

100 g/7 tablespoons butter, melted

FOR THE FILLING

500 g/generous 2 cups mascarpone cheese

500 ml/2 cups crème fraîche

3 generous tablespoons icing/
confectioners' sugar, or to taste

grated zest of 2 lemons

*a 20-cm/8-inch square loose-based cake
pan, greased and lined*

SERVES 10

Begin by making the blueberry topping. Simmer the blueberries with the lemon juice and sugar in a saucepan for about 5 minutes until the fruit has burst and you have a thick sauce. Set aside to cool.

To make the crumb base, crush the biscuits/graham crackers to fine crumbs in a food processor or place in a clean plastic bag and bash with a rolling pin. Transfer the crumbs to a mixing bowl and stir in the melted butter. Press the buttery crumbs into the base of the prepared cake pan firmly using the back of a spoon.

To make the filling, whisk together the mascarpone and crème fraîche in a large mixing bowl until smooth. Sift in the icing/confectioners' sugar, add the lemon zest, then whisk again. Taste the mixture and add a little more icing/confectioners' sugar if you wish it to be sweeter.

Spoon the filling mixture over the crumb base and level with a knife or spatula, then spoon the blueberry topping over the top. Chill the cheesecake in the refrigerator for at least 3 hours or until set, then cut into slices to serve.

raspberry ripple cheesecake

Raspberry ripple is a popular ice cream flavour – vanilla ice cream with ribbons of raspberry syrup swirled through. It is a perfect combination for a cheesecake and you can create a pretty pattern on top by swirling the raspberry sauce with a fork. Top with extra fresh raspberries, if you wish, for an extra treat.

FOR THE RASPBERRY RIPPLE SAUCE

125 g/1 cup raspberries

100 g/½ cup caster/white sugar

FOR THE CRUMB BASE

150 g/5½ oz. digestive biscuits/
graham crackers

90 g/6 tablespoons butter, melted

125 g/1 cup raspberries

FOR THE FILLING

250 g/generous 1 cup mascarpone cheese

250 ml/1 cup crème fraîche

2 tablespoons icing/confectioners'
sugar, or to taste

1 teaspoon vanilla bean paste

an 18-cm/7-inch round loose-based cake
pan, 5 cm/2 inches deep, greased and lined

SERVES 8

Begin by preparing the ripple sauce as this needs to chill before being swirled in the cheesecake. Simmer the raspberries and sugar with 60 ml/¼ cup water for about 5 minutes until syrupy, then pass through a fine mesh sieve/strainer to remove the seeds and set aside to cool.

To make the crumb base, crush the biscuits/graham crackers to fine crumbs in a food processor or place in a clean plastic bag and bash with a rolling pin. Transfer the crumbs to a mixing bowl and stir in the melted butter. Press the buttery crumbs into the base of the prepared cake pan firmly using the back of a spoon. Arrange two thirds of the raspberries for the base in a ring around the edge of the pan, then sprinkle the rest out over the centre of the base.

For the filling, whisk together the mascarpone and crème fraîche in a large mixing bowl until smooth, sift over the icing/confectioners' sugar, add the vanilla bean paste and whisk again. Taste for sweetness, adding a little more icing/confectioners' sugar if necessary.

Drizzle a little of the raspberry sauce over the raspberries on the base, then pour half of the sauce into the filling mixture and gently fold through until the mixture has thin ribbons of raspberry sauce running through it. Do not over mix or you will lose the pretty ripple effect.

Spoon the filling mixture over the crumb base. Place spoonfuls of the remaining raspberry sauce on top of the cheesecake a small distance apart, then swirl them through the mixture using a fork or a knife to make a pretty ripple pattern. Chill in the refrigerator for at least 3 hours until the cheesecake has set.

New York cheesecake

With my brother living in Brooklyn, New York cheesecake has always had a special place in my heart. It may be simple, just flavoured with vanilla, but a slice of this is a pure indulgence. There are many recipes for New York cheesecake, and many bakeries claiming to sell the original. This is my take: purists among you, don't judge the English addition of clotted cream – it works very well, I promise!

FOR THE CRUMB BASE

150 g/5½ oz. digestive biscuits/graham crackers

90 g/6 tablespoons butter, melted

FOR THE FILLING

600 g/2⅔ cups cream cheese

225 g/1 cup clotted cream (if unavailable, use crème fraîche)

100 ml/generous ⅓ cup crème fraîche

140 g/¾ cup caster/white sugar

4 eggs

1 teaspoon vanilla bean paste

FOR THE TOPPING

300 ml/1¼ cups sour cream

3 tablespoons icing/confectioners' sugar

a 26-cm/10-inch round springform cake pan, greased and lined

SERVES 12

Preheat the oven to 170°C (325°F) Gas 3.

To make the crumb base, crush the biscuits/graham crackers to fine crumbs in a food processor or place in a clean plastic bag and bash with a rolling pin. Transfer the crumbs to a mixing bowl and stir in the melted butter. Press the buttery crumbs into the base of the prepared cake pan firmly using the back of a spoon. Wrap the outside of the pan in cling film/plastic wrap and place in a roasting pan half full with water, ensuring that the water is not so high as to spill out. Set aside.

For the filling, whisk together the cream cheese, clotted cream, crème fraîche, sugar, eggs and vanilla bean paste in a blender or with an electric whisk. Pour the mixture over the crumb base, then transfer the cheesecake, in its waterbath, to the preheated oven and bake for 45–60 minutes until the cheesecake is set but still wobbles slightly. Remove the cheesecake from the oven and allow it to cool slightly so that the height of the cheesecake reduces. Leave the oven on.

To make the topping, whisk together the sour cream and icing/confectioners' sugar and pour over the top of the cheesecake. Return to the oven and bake for a further 10–15 minutes until set.

Remove the cheesecake from the waterbath and slide a knife around the edge of the pan to release the cheesecake and prevent it from cracking. Leave to cool completely in the pan, then chill in the refrigerator for at least 3 hours before serving.

lemon and ginger cheesecake

Lemon and ginger are the perfect pick-me-up combination. This cheesecake is flavoured with delicate ginger syrup and studded with piquant stem ginger pieces, which contrast with the tangy lemon curd that is swirled on top of the cheesecake. A fantastic dessert for ginger lovers.

FOR THE CRUMB CASE

300 g/10½ oz. ginger biscuits/cookies

150 g/1¼ sticks butter, melted

FOR THE TOPPING

60 g/4 tablespoons butter

freshly squeezed juice and grated zest of 3 lemons

100 g/½ cup caster/white sugar

3 large egg yolks

FOR THE FILLING

6 sheets leaf gelatine

300 g/1⅓ cups cream cheese

250 g/generous 1 cup mascarpone cheese

100 g/½ cup caster/white sugar

4 balls preserved stem ginger, finely chopped

60 ml/¼ cup ginger syrup (from the preserved stem ginger jar)

250 ml/1 cup double/heavy cream

a 23-cm/9-inch round springform cake pan, greased and lined

SERVES 12

Begin by preparing the lemon curd topping. Put the butter, lemon juice and sugar in a heatproof bowl set over a pan of simmering water. Whisk until the sugar has dissolved then remove from the heat and set aside to cool slightly. Whisk in the egg yolks and lemon zest, then return the bowl to the pan over the water and stir all the time until the curd thickens. Leave to cool completely.

For the crumb case, crush the ginger biscuits/cookies to fine crumbs in a food processor or place in a clean plastic bag and bash with a rolling pin. Transfer the crumbs to a mixing bowl and stir in the melted butter. Press the buttery crumbs into the base and sides of the prepared cake pan firmly using the back of a spoon. You need the crumbs to come up about 3–4 cm/1½ inches high on the side of the pan so that they make a case for the filling.

To make the filling, soak the gelatine leaves in water until they are soft.

In a large mixing bowl, whisk together the cream cheese, mascarpone and sugar until light and creamy, then beat in the chopped ginger pieces.

Put the ginger syrup and 120 ml/½ cup water in a heatproof bowl set over a saucepan of simmering water and heat gently. Squeeze the water out of the gelatine leaves and add them to the warm ginger syrup, stirring until the gelatine has dissolved. Carefully add the ginger syrup to the cream cheese mixture, passing it through a sieve/strainer as you go to remove any undissolved gelatine pieces. Add the double/heavy cream and whisk everything together until the mixture is smooth and slightly thick.

Pour the filling into the crumb case and tap it gently so that the mixture is even, then chill in the refrigerator for 3 hours or overnight.

Before serving, place spoonfuls of the lemon curd on top of the cheese filling and swirl them gently using a knife to make pretty patterns.

mini chocolate chip cheesecakes

These little cheesecakes with a choc chip topping and salty chocolate pretzel base are just too tempting to resist – they are my favourite cheesecake recipe! For an extra special treat you can serve them with ice cream and hot chocolate sauce if you wish.

FOR THE CRUMB BASES

100 g/3½ oz. Oreo cookies

50 g/2 oz. pretzels

70 g/5 tablespoons butter, melted

FOR THE FILLING

250 g/generous 1 cup cream cheese

250 g/generous 1 cup ricotta

2 small eggs

1 teaspoon vanilla bean paste

200 g/scant 1 cup condensed milk

200 g/1¼ cups chocolate chunks (milk, white, dark, or mixture of your choice)

a 12-hole loose-based mini cheesecake pan/muffin pan, greased

MAKES 12

Preheat the oven to 170°C (325°F) Gas 3.

To make the bases, crush the Oreos and pretzels to very fine crumbs in a food processor or place in a clean plastic bag and bash with a rolling pin. Transfer the crumbs to a mixing bowl and stir in the melted butter. Put a spoonful of the crumbs into each hole of the prepared pan and press down firmly using the end of a rolling pin or the back of a small spoon.

For the filling, whisk together the cream cheese and ricotta in a large mixing bowl. Add the eggs, vanilla bean paste and condensed milk and whisk again until smooth, then stir in three quarters of the chocolate chips.

Pour the filling mixture into the 12 holes of the pan leaving a little space in each hole as the cheesecakes will expand slightly during cooking. (Depending on the size of your pan, you may not need all of the mixture.) Bake in the preheated oven for 20–25 minutes until set with a slight wobble. Sprinkle over the remaining chocolate chips straight away so that they melt slightly on the warm cheesecakes, then leave to cool. Once cool, remove from the pan and chill in the refrigerator for 3 hours before serving.

fruits of the forest cheesecake bars

Fruits of the forest cheesecake is the ultimate 1970s throwback. I remember it being one of my favourite desserts as a child. This is my version, served in individual rectangular portions made in a silicone mould and topped with fresh berries and a drizzle of coulis. If you do not have this shape mould you can make the cheesecake in a loaf pan and then cut into slices once frozen. You can serve these cheesecakes fully defrosted or semi frozen for a fruity semifreddo dessert.

FOR THE CRUMB BASES

120 g/4 oz. digestive biscuits/graham crackers

70 g/5 tablespoons butter, melted

FOR THE FILLING

300 g/10½ oz. frozen fruits of the forest

75 g/scant ½ cup caster/white sugar, or to taste

250 g/generous 1 cup mascarpone cheese

250 ml/1 cup crème fraîche

250 g/2 cups berries (blackberries, raspberries, strawberries), for the topping

a 12-cell silicone cake bar mould (each hole 8 x 3 cm/3 x 1½ inches)

MAKES 12

Preheat the oven to 180°C (350°F) Gas 4.

To make the crumb bases, crush the biscuits/graham crackers to fine crumbs in a food processor or place in a clean plastic bag and bash with a rolling pin. Transfer the crumbs to a mixing bowl and stir in the melted butter. Press the buttery crumbs into the base of each hole of the silicone mould firmly using the back of a spoon, then bake in the preheated oven for 10–12 minutes. Leave to cool completely.

For the cheesecake filling, put the fruit and sugar in a saucepan with 60 ml/¼ cup water and simmer until the mixture is thick and syrupy. Test the berries for sweetness and add a little extra sugar if you wish. Pass through a sieve/strainer to remove the seeds, then leave to cool completely. Reserve a few spoonfuls of this fruit coulis to drizzle over the cheesecakes when serving.

In a large mixing bowl, whisk together the mascarpone and crème fraîche, then fold in the remaining fruit coulis. Taste for sweetness and add a little more sugar if it is not sweet enough. Spoon over the crumb bases in the mould, then transfer to the freezer. Leave until set, then pop the bars of cheesecake out of the mould. Place on serving plates and leave to defrost. When you are ready to serve, arrange berries on top of each cheesecake and drizzle with the reserved coulis.

coffee cheesecakes

These boozy little coffee cups are the perfect end to supper – combining dessert, liqueur and after dinner coffee all in one. I have used a coffee liqueur to soak the biscuits/cookies in, but amaretto or Baileys would also work well, if you prefer.

FOR THE CRUMB BASES

80 g/3 oz. amaretti biscuits/cookies

80 ml/⅓ cup espresso coffee*, cooled

coffee liqueur (such as Tia Maria or Kahlua), to drizzle

FOR THE FILLING

4 sheets leaf gelatine

200 g/scant 1 cup cream cheese

200 g/scant 1 cup mascarpone cheese

100 g/½ cup caster/white sugar

160 ml/⅔ cup double/heavy cream

80 ml/⅓ cup espresso coffee*, cooled

1 tablespoon coffee liqueur

TO ASSEMBLE

160 ml/⅔ cup double/heavy cream

1 tablespoon coffee liqueur

cocoa powder, to dust

6 or 12 chocolate coffee beans

6 glasses or 12 espresso cups

MAKES 6 OR 12

*If you don't have an espresso machine, dissolve 1 tablespoon coffee granules in 80 ml/⅓ cup hot water, then leave to cool before using in the recipe.

For the bases, crush the amaretti biscuits/cookies into small pieces with your hands or using a rolling pin. Divide between the glasses or espresso cups and drizzle a little espresso and a little liqueur into the base of each.

For the filling, soak the gelatine leaves in water until they are soft.

In a large mixing bowl, whisk together the cream cheese, mascarpone and sugar until light and creamy.

Put the cream and espresso in a heatproof bowl set over a pan of simmering water and heat gently. Squeeze the water out of the gelatine leaves, add them to the warm cream and stir until dissolved. Pass the coffee cream through a sieve/strainer to remove any undissolved gelatine pieces, then whisk into the cheese mixture along with the coffee liqueur. Spoon the cheesecake filling into the glasses or espresso cups and leave to set in the refrigerator for 3 hours or overnight.

When you are ready to serve, whip the double/heavy cream and coffee liqueur together to stiff peaks. Spoon equally over the tops of the cheesecakes and dust with cocoa powder, finishing with a chocolate coffee bean.

peach melba cheesecake

The classic ice cream dessert – peach melba – is the inspiration for this cheesecake. The original is said to have been created for the famous soprano Dame Nellie Melba, served with ice cream to soothe her voice. Bursting with juicy peaches and fresh berries, I am sure she would have approved of this cheesecake. Serve with scoops of vanilla ice cream to accompany, if you wish.

FOR THE CRUMB CASE

300 g/10½ cups malted milk biscuits/cookies

150 g/1¼ sticks butter, melted

125 g/1 cup raspberries

FOR THE FILLING

4 sheets leaf gelatine

4 ripe peaches, pitted

100 g/½ cup caster/white sugar

200 g/scant 1 cup cream cheese

250 g/generous 1 cup ricotta

150 ml/⅔ cup double/heavy cream

FOR THE TOPPING

1 packet glaze topping/fixing gel (such as Dr. Oetker)
OR
2 sheets leaf gelatine, freshly squeezed juice of 2 lemons and 30 g/ 2½ tablespoons caster/white sugar

3 ripe peaches

125 g/1 cup raspberries

a 23-cm/9-inch round springform cake pan, greased and lined

SERVES 12

To make the crumb case, crush the biscuits/cookies to fine crumbs in a food processor or place in a clean plastic bag and bash with a rolling pin. Transfer the crumbs to a mixing bowl and stir in the melted butter. Press the buttery crumbs into the base and sides of the prepared cake pan firmly using the back of a spoon. You need the crumbs to come up about 3–4 cm/1½ inches high on the side of the pan so that they make a case for the filling. Sprinkle the raspberries over the base.

For the filling, soak the gelatine leaves in water until they are soft. Purée the peaches until smooth in a blender or food processor.

In a large mixing bowl, whisk together the sugar, cream cheese and ricotta until light and creamy.

Put the double/heavy cream in a heatproof bowl set over a pan of simmering water and heat the cream until it is just warm. Squeeze the water out of the gelatine leaves and add them to the warm cream, stirring until dissolved. Pass the cream through a sieve/strainer to remove any undissolved gelatine pieces, then whisk into the cheese mixture. Fold in the peach purée, then pour the filling into the crumb case and smooth level.

For the glaze, if using a packet glaze, prepare according to the packet instructions. If making your own glaze, soak the gelatine leaves in water until softened. In a saucepan, gently heat the lemon juice and sugar with 250 ml/1 cup water until the sugar has dissolved and the liquid is warm but not boiling. Squeeze the water from the gelatine leaves and add them to the pan, stirring until dissolved (Do not boil the liquid as this will cause the gelatine to lose its setting properties.) Pass the glaze through a sieve/ strainer, then leave until just cool but not set.

Cut the peaches for the topping into thin slices and arrange on top of the cheesecake. Sprinkle over the raspberries and then carefully pour over the cooled glaze. Leave to set in the refrigerator overnight.

rum and raisin cheesecakes

Rum and raisin is one of those 'love or hate' combinations. I have used spiced rum, which has delicious hints of vanilla and cinnamon. If you have only regular dark rum available, you can add a little ground cinnamon to the cheesecake mixture if you wish. Served with a buttery rum syrup and extra raisins, these are the perfect individual dessert cheesecakes. For an almond variation, you can replace the rum with amaretto and use amaretti biscuits/cookies in place of half of the digestive biscuits/graham crackers.

FOR THE FILLING

150 g/1 cup mixed raisins (golden, flame and green)

250 ml/1 cup spiced rum (or ordinary dark rum if not available)

250 g/generous 1 cup cream cheese

250 g/generous 1 cup ricotta

2 small eggs

1 tablespoon dark brown sugar

60 g/⅓ cup caster/white sugar

FOR THE CRUMB BASES

150 g/5½ oz. chocolate digestive biscuits/graham crackers

75 g/5 tablespoons butter, melted

FOR THE RUM SAUCE

100 g/7 tablespoons butter

100 g/½ cup caster/white sugar

160 ml/⅔ cup double/heavy cream

a 12-hole loose-based cheesecake pan/muffin tin, greased

MAKES 12

The day before you wish to make the cheesecakes, put the raisins and the rum in a bowl together, cover and leave to soak overnight.

Preheat the oven to 170°C (325°F) Gas 3.

To make the crumb bases, crush the chocolate biscuits/graham crackers to fine crumbs in a food processor or place in a clean plastic bag and bash with a rolling pin. Transfer the crumbs to a mixing bowl and stir in the melted butter. Place a spoonful of the crumbs into each hole of the prepared cheesecake pan and press down firmly using the end of a rolling pin or the back of a small spoon.

For the filling, whisk together the cream cheese and ricotta in a large mixing bowl. Add the eggs, sugars, half of the rum-soaked raisins and 2 tablespoons of the soaking rum and whisk again until smooth. Spoon the mixture into the 12 holes of the pan so that they are almost full. (Depending on the size of your pan, you may not need all of the mixture.) Bake the cheesecakes in the preheated oven for about 20–25 minutes until set with a slight wobble in the centre. Leave to cool, then chill in the refrigerator until you are ready to serve.

For the rum sauce, simmer the butter and sugar together in a saucepan until the sugar has dissolved. Add the cream and simmer for a few minutes. Remove from the heat and stir in the remaining rum and raisins, then set aside to cool.

Serve the cheesecakes chilled with a small jug/pitcher of rum sauce on the side for drizzling.

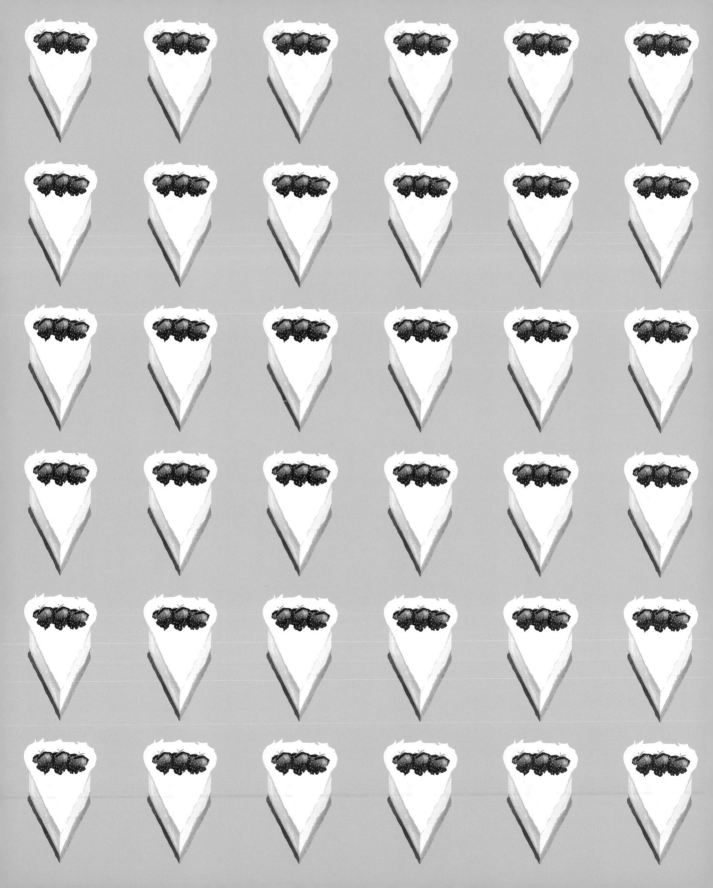

fruity cheesecakes

glazed fruit cheesecake

This cheesecake reminds me of the classic fruit tarts that often line the windows of French pâtisseries. You can top the cheesecake with any fruits of your choosing. The base is made of one of my favourite biscuits/cookies – the humble British custard cream – which has a delicious vanilla flavour cream in the middle. There is a good variety of fixing gel mixes that you can purchase in supermarkets that make glazing the tart very easy and give a very professional result. If you are not able to find these, I have included a recipe for making a glaze yourself.

FOR THE CRUMB BASE

200 g/7 oz. custard cream biscuits/cookies

100 g/7 tablespoons butter, melted

FOR THE FILLING

4 sheets leaf gelatine

200 g/scant 1 cup cream cheese

250 g/generous 1 cup quark/farmer cheese

100 g/½ cup caster/white sugar

250 ml/1 cup double/heavy cream

1 vanilla pod/bean

FOR THE TOPPING

fresh fruit of your choice (mango, grapes, strawberries, raspberries, blueberries, redcurrants)

1 packet glaze topping/fixing gel (such as Dr. Oetker)
OR
2 sheets leaf gelatine, freshly squeezed juice of 2 lemons and 30 g/ 2½ tablespoons caster/white sugar

a 23-cm/9-inch round springform cake pan, greased and lined

SERVES 10

To make the crumb base, crush the custard creams to fine crumbs in a food processor or place in a clean plastic bag and bash with a rolling pin. Transfer the crumbs to a mixing bowl and stir in the melted butter. Press the buttery crumbs into the base of the prepared cake pan firmly using the back of a spoon.

For the filling, soak the gelatine leaves in water until they are soft.

In a large mixing bowl, whisk together the cream cheese, quark/farmer cheese and sugar until light and creamy.

Put the cream in a heatproof bowl. Split the vanilla pod/bean and remove the seeds with the back of a knife. Add the seeds and the pod to the cream and set the bowl over a pan of simmering water to heat gently. When warm, remove the pod/bean (you can wash and dry it, then store in a jar of sugar to make vanilla sugar). Squeeze the water out of the gelatine leaves and add them to the warm vanilla cream, stirring until dissolved. Pass the cream through a sieve/strainer to remove any undissolved gelatine pieces, then whisk into the cheesecake mixture. Pour the mixture over the crumb base and chill in the refrigerator for an hour.

For the topping, place the fruit in a pretty arrangement on top of the cheesecake. Prepare the glaze according to the packet instructions and pour over the cheesecake. If you are making your own glaze, soak the gelatine leaves in cold water. Heat the lemon juice in a saucepan with 250 ml/1 cup water and the sugar until the sugar has dissolved and the mixture is warm but not boiling (having the liquid too hot will affect the setting properties of the gelatine). Squeeze the water out of the gelatine leaves, add them to the pan and stir in until dissolved. Pass the glaze through a sieve/strainer, then leave until just cool but not set. Pour the glaze over the fruit, then leave the cheesecake to set in the refrigerator overnight before serving.

champagne rhubarb cheesecake

I love rhubarb. Its season is short so you need to make the most of this delicious fruit whilst it is around. This cheesecake is topped with kitsch crispy cornflakes – a perfect contrast to the sharp rhubarb. The cheesecake filling is delicately flavoured with hints of ginger, which really bring out the flavour of the rhubarb. If you are not able to find pink rhubarb, you can add a few drops of pink food colouring if you wish.

FOR THE FRUIT

850 g/1 lb. 10 oz. pink champagne rhubarb

80 ml/⅓ cup ginger syrup

50 g/¼ cup caster/white sugar

FOR THE CRUMB CASE

300 g/10½ oz. ginger biscuits/cookies

150 g/1¼ sticks butter, melted

FOR THE FILLING

4 sheets leaf gelatine

200 g/scant 1 cup cream cheese

250 g/generous 1 cup quark/ farmer cheese

30 g/2½ tablespoons caster/white sugar

180 ml/¾ cup double/heavy cream

FOR THE TOPPING

1 tablespoons butter

1 tablespoon golden/light corn syrup

30 g/generous 1 cup cornflakes

a 23-cm/9-inch round springform cake pan, greased and lined

a silicone mat (optional)

SERVES 10

Preheat the oven to 180°C (350°F) Gas 4.

Peel the rhubarb, cut it into 7-cm/3-inch lengths and place in a roasting pan. Drizzle over the ginger syrup and sprinkle with the sugar. (You do not need to add any water as a lot of juice will be released from the rhubarb.) Bake in the preheated oven for 15–20 minutes until the fruit is soft but still holds its shape. Remove from the oven and leave to cool. Purée half of the fruit in a food processor and reserve the remainder for the topping.

To make the crumb case, crush the biscuits/cookies to fine crumbs in a food processor or place in a clean plastic bag and bash with a rolling pin. Transfer the crumbs to a mixing bowl and stir in the melted butter. Press the buttery crumbs into the base and sides of the prepared cake pan firmly using the back of a spoon. You need the crumbs to come up about 3–4 cm/1½ inches high on the side of the pan so that they make a case for the filling.

For the filling, soak the gelatine leaves in water until they are soft. In a large mixing bowl, whisk together the cream cheese, quark/farmer cheese and sugar until light and creamy, then add the puréed rhubarb and fold it through.

Put the double/heavy cream in a heatproof bowl set over a pan of simmering water and heat gently. Squeeze the water out of the gelatine leaves and add them to the warmed cream, stirring until dissolved. Pass the cream through a sieve/strainer to remove any undissolved gelatine pieces, then whisk into the cheese mixture. Pour the mixture into the crumb case and leave to set in the refrigerator for 3 hours or overnight.

For the topping, melt the butter and syrup together in a large saucepan, then stir in the cornflakes, making sure that each flake is well coated. Spread the flakes out on a silicone mat or sheet of non-stick baking paper and leave to set.

When you are ready to serve, remove the cheesecake from the pan and place on a serving plate. Arrange the rhubarb pieces on top of the cheesecake and sprinkle with the cornflakes (don't be tempted to do this in advance or the cornflakes will become soggy).

lemon meringue cheesecake

If I had to pick one dish that I remember from my childhood it is my mum's lemon meringue pie. She would often make it for dinner parties and my brother and I would be saved a slice to eat for breakfast the next day. With giant layers of fluffy meringue and tangy lemon cream, it is still one of my favourite desserts today and we always ask Mum to make it when we go for Sunday lunch. This is my cheesecake interpretation!

FOR THE CRUMB CASE

300 g/10½ oz. digestive biscuits/graham crackers

150 g/1¼ sticks butter, melted

4 tablespoons/¼ cup lemon curd

FOR THE FILLING

6 sheets leaf gelatine

300 g/1⅓ cups cream cheese

250 g/generous 1 cup ricotta

150 ml/⅔ cup sour cream

100 g/½ cup caster/white sugar

freshly squeezed juice and grated zest of 2 lemons

FOR THE MERINGUE TOPPING

150 g/¾ cup caster/superfine sugar

60 ml/¼ cup light corn syrup (or golden syrup if not available)

3 egg whites

a 23-cm/9-inch round springform cake pan, greased and lined

a piping bag fitted with a large round nozzle/tip

a chef's blow torch (optional)

SERVES 10

To make the crumb case, crush the biscuits/graham crackers to fine crumbs in a food processor or place in a clean plastic bag and bash with a rolling pin. Transfer the crumbs to a mixing bowl and stir in the melted butter. Press the buttery crumbs into the base and sides of the prepared cake pan firmly using the back of a spoon. You need the crumbs to come up about 3–4 cm/1½ inches high on the side of the pan so that they make a case for the filling. Spoon the lemon curd over the base of the crust and spread out gently into an even layer with a spoon.

For the filling, soak the gelatine leaves in water until they are soft.

In a large mixing bowl, whisk together the cream cheese, ricotta, sour cream and sugar until light and creamy, then stir in the lemon zest.

Put the lemon juice and 60 ml/¼ cup water in a heatproof bowl set over a pan of simmering water and heat gently. Squeeze the water out of the gelatine leaves and add them to the warm lemon juice, stirring until the gelatine has dissolved. Pass the lemon jelly through a sieve/strainer to remove any undissolved gelatine pieces, then add it to the cream cheese mixture and beat until it is smooth and slightly thick. Pour the filling into the crumb case and chill in the refrigerator for 3–4 hours or overnight until set.

For the meringue topping, heat the sugar, syrup and 4 tablespoons water in a saucepan until the sugar has dissolved, then bring to the boil. Whisk the egg whites with a balloon whisk or mixer until they form stiff peaks. Gradually pour the hot sugar syrup into the egg whites in a thin stream and continue whisking until the meringue cools down and is glossy and firm. This will take about 10 minutes and is therefore best done with a stand mixer.

Spoon the meringue into the piping bag and pipe the meringue onto the cheesecake in high peaks. Lightly brown the meringue with a chef's blow torch or under a hot grill/broiler. Store in the refrigerator if you are not serving at once.

mini baked blueberry cheesecakes

These are perfect picnic cheesecakes as you can seal the jars and transport them easily.
I have flavoured these with blueberries and vanilla but you can substitute a variety of other
flavours – lemon zest, a shot of espresso coffee or chocolate chips – if you prefer.

FOR THE CRUMB BASES

130 g/4½ oz. digestive biscuits/
graham crackers

60 g/4 tablespoons butter, melted

FOR THE FILLING

250 g/generous 1 cup mascarpone cheese

300 ml/1¼ cups sour cream

2 eggs

70 g/⅓ cup caster/white sugar

1 teaspoon vanilla bean paste

100 g/¾ cup blueberries

6 small kilner jars or jam jars

MAKES 6

Preheat the oven to 170°C (325°F) Gas 3.

To make the crumb bases, crush the biscuits/graham crackers to fine crumbs in a food processor or place in a clean plastic bag and bash with a rolling pin. Transfer the crumbs to a mixing bowl and stir in the melted butter. Divide the buttery crumbs between the jars and press down firmly with a spoon or the end of a rolling pin.

For the filling, whisk together the mascarpone cheese, sour cream, eggs, sugar and vanilla bean paste in a large mixing bowl until thick and creamy. Pour the filling carefully into the jars, then sprinkle the blueberries evenly over the tops of the cheesecakes.

Place the jars in a large roasting pan half full with water, ensuring that the water is not so high as to spill out or go over the top of the cheesecake jars. Transfer the cheesecakes, in their waterbath, to the preheated oven and bake for about 25–30 minutes until just set but still with a slight wobble in the centre. Leave to cool, then chill in the refrigerator until you are ready to serve.

key lime pie cheesecake

This recipe is adapted from a recipe given to me by my good friend Bree for her family's lemon cheesecake. No bake, no fuss, this is quick and easy and very delicious. Bree was in my first heat on Masterchef and it was a close call as to whether she or I went through – this cheesecake therefore has high credentials!

FOR THE CRUMB CASE

300 g/10½ oz. digestive biscuits/graham crackers

150 g/1¼ sticks butter, melted

FOR THE FILLING

6 limes

600 g/2⅔ cups cream cheese

400 g/1¾ cups condensed milk

FOR THE CANDIED LIME ZEST

70 g/⅓ cup caster/white sugar

long grated zest of 4 of the limes (see method)

200 ml/¾ cup double/heavy cream, whipped, for the topping

a 23-cm/9-inch round springform cake pan, greased and lined

a piping bag fitted with a large star nozzle/tip

SERVES 10

Preheat the oven to 180°C (350°F) Gas 4.

To make the crumb case, crush the biscuits/graham crackers to fine crumbs in a food processor or place in a clean plastic bag and bash with a rolling pin. Transfer the crumbs to a mixing bowl and stir in the melted butter. Press the buttery crumbs into the base and sides of the prepared cake pan firmly using the back of a spoon. You need the crumbs to come up about 3 cm/1 inch high on the side of the pan so that they make a case for the filling. Bake the crumb case in the oven for 5–8 minutes, then leave to cool completely.

For the candied lime zest, pare the zest of 4 of the limes into long thin strips. Simmer the long strips of lime zest with the sugar and 60 ml/¼ cup water for about 5 minutes until you have a thin syrup. Remove the lime zest from the pan and place on a wire rack to drain and cool.

For the filling, finely grate the zest of the 2 remaining limes, and juice all 6 limes.

In a large mixing bowl, whisk together the cream cheese, condensed milk, finely grated lime zest and the lime juice until smooth. Spoon the mixture into the crumb case and chill in the refrigerator for at least 3 hours until the cheesecake has set.

When you are ready to serve, spoon the whipped cream into the piping bag and pipe large cream stars around the edge of the cheesecake. Decorate with the candied lime zest.

tropical coconut cheesecake

This is a light and delicate cheesecake that will transport you beachside. Full of flavour and bright sunshine colours, this is a perfect summer dessert. You can use dried, fresh or canned pineapple for the topping – soaked in coconut rum, they all taste nice!

FOR THE CRUMB CASE

300 g/10½ oz. coconut ring biscuits/cookies

150 g/1¼ sticks butter, melted

50 g/⅔ cup long soft shredded coconut

FOR THE FILLING

6 sheets leaf gelatine

300 g/1⅓ cups cream cheese

250 g/generous 1 cup mascarpone cheese

100 g/½ cup vanilla sugar or 100 g/ ½ cup caster/white sugar plus 1 teaspoon vanilla extract

400 ml/1¾ cups coconut milk

250 ml/1 cup double/heavy cream

1 tablespoon coconut rum (such as Malibu)

FOR THE TOPPING

1 pineapple, peeled

60 ml/¼ cup coconut rum (such as Malibu)

50 g/⅔ cup coconut flakes

a 23-cm/9-inch round springform cake pan, greased and lined

a silicone mat (optional)

SERVES 12

To make the crumb case, crush the coconut biscuits/cookies to fine crumbs in a food processor or place in a clean plastic bag and bash with a rolling pin. Transfer the crumbs to a mixing bowl and stir in the melted butter and shredded coconut. Press the mixture into the base and sides of the prepared cake pan firmly with the back of a spoon. You need the crumbs to come up about 3–4 cm/1½ inches high on the side of the pan so that they make a case for the filling.

For the filling, soak the gelatine leaves in water until they are soft.

In a large mixing bowl, whisk together the cream cheese, mascarpone and vanilla sugar until light and creamy.

Put the coconut milk and double/heavy cream in a heatproof bowl set over a saucepan of simmering water and heat gently. Squeeze the water from the gelatine leaves and stir them into the warm cream until the gelatine has dissolved. Pass through a sieve/strainer to remove any undissolved gelatine pieces, then whisk the cream into the cheese mixture along with the rum. Spoon the filling into the crumb case and chill in the refrigerator for 3–4 hours or overnight until set.

To make the pineapple topping, preheat the oven to 120°C (250°F) Gas ½. Slice the peeled pineapple very thinly and lay the slices on a silicone mat or sheet of baking parchment. Bake in the preheated oven for about 1½–2 hours until the pineapple is dried but not brown. (The actual cooking time will depend on the thickness of your pineapple slices.) Leave the pineapple to cool, then place the slices in a shallow dish and pour over the coconut rum. Cover and leave to soak for at least 1 hour.

Toast the coconut in a dry frying pan, stirring all the time to make sure that it does not burn, then leave to cool.

When you are ready to serve, drain the pineapple of any excess liquid and arrange over the top of the cheesecake, leaving a border around the edge. Sprinkle the toasted coconut flakes around the edge of the cheesecake and serve.

cheesecake charlotte

Topped with fresh summer berries, served drizzled with a berry coulis and tied with a beautiful ribbon, this cheesecake twist on the classic charlotte makes an elegant dessert for a special occasion. To make an autumn charlotte you can replace the berries with drained poached pears and blackberries for equally delicious results.

FOR THE CRUMB BASE

200 g/7 oz. digestive biscuits/graham crackers

100 g/7 tablespoons butter, melted

FOR THE FILLING

250 g/generous 1 cup mascarpone cheese

300 ml/1¼ cups crème fraîche

3 tablespoons icing/confectioners' sugar

1 vanilla pod/bean, split

finely grated zest of 1 lemon

FOR THE STRAWBERRY SAUCE

300 g/2½–3 cups strawberries

100 g/½ cup caster/white sugar

TO ASSEMBLE

200 g/7 oz. Savoiardi biscuits (sponge fingers/ladyfinger cookies)

200 g/1½–1⅔ cups blueberries

200 g/1½–1⅔ cups raspberries

400 g/3½–4 cups strawberries

an 18-cm/7-inch round springform cake pan, greased and lined

pretty ribbon, to decorate

SERVES 8

To make the crumb base, crush the biscuits/graham crackers to fine crumbs in a food processor or place in a clean plastic bag and bash with a rolling pin. Transfer the crumbs to a mixing bowl and stir in the melted butter. Press the buttery crumbs into the base of the prepared cake pan firmly using the back of a spoon.

For the filling, whisk together the mascarpone cheese, crème fraîche, icing/confectioners' sugar, seeds scraped out of the vanilla pod/bean (reserve the pod/bean for later) and lemon zest in a large mixing bowl until smooth. Spoon the mixture over the crumb base, level the top of the cheesecake and chill in the refrigerator until set, preferably overnight.

Whilst the cheesecake is chilling, prepare the strawberry sauce by simmering the strawberries, sugar and the deseeded vanilla pod/bean in a saucepan with 80 ml/⅓ cup water until the fruit is very soft and the liquid is syrupy. Pass the mixture through a sieve/strainer pressing out all the juice from the strawberries, then discard the pressed fruit. Set aside to cool.

When you are ready to serve, remove the cheesecake from the pan by sliding a round-bladed knife around the edge of the pan to release the cheesecake, then place on a serving plate. Cut a quarter from one end of each sponge finger/ladyfinger so that that end is now flat rather than rounded, and arrange them upright and touching, in a standing ring around the sides of the cheesecake, with the rounded ends uppermost. The Savoiardi should come up at least 3 cm/1 inch above the top of the cheesecake so that they create a wall to contain the fruit. Tie the ribbon tightly around the cheesecake to hold the Savoiardi in place. Arrange the fruit on top of the cheesecake, then use a pastry brush to brush a little of the strawberry sauce over the fruit to glaze. Serve with the remaining strawberry sauce to pour over the cheesecake.

Note: Don't be tempted to pour all of the sauce over the top of the cheesecake as it will drip down through the Savoiardi and leak onto the ribbon and serving plate. Simply decant the remaining sauce into a jug/pitcher and serve on the side.

plum crumble cheesecake

Plum crumble is one of my favourite desserts. My mum makes the best crumble and we always finish the whole dish whenever she makes it. This cheesecake is light and tangy – bursting with the flavours of the plum purée. With crumble on the base and on top of the cheesecake and cinnamon-roasted plums, this is a great summer dessert to serve when plums are in season.

FOR THE TOPPING

800 g/1¾ lbs. red plums

50 g/¼ cup caster/white sugar

2 teaspoons ground cinnamon

FOR THE CRUMBLE

160 g/1½ sticks butter

200 g/1½ cups self-raising flour

100 g/½ cup granulated sugar

2 teaspoons ground cinnamon

FOR THE FILLING

5 sheets leaf gelatine

300 g/1⅓ cups cream cheese

250 g/generous 1 cup ricotta

100 g/½ cup caster/white sugar

250 ml/1 cup double/heavy cream

a 23-cm/9-inch round springform cake pan, greased and lined

SERVES 12

Begin by preparing the plum topping. Preheat the oven to 180°C (350°F) Gas 4. Cut the plums in half and remove the stones/pits. Place the plums cut side down in a roasting pan. Sprinkle with the sugar and cinnamon and add 100 ml/⅓ cup water to the pan. Bake the plums in the preheated oven for 20–25 minutes or until soft, then set aside to cool. Reserve 12 baked plum halves and the baking juice from the pan for the topping and purée the remaining plums in a food processor. (Leave the oven on for cooking the crumble.)

Prepare the crumble by rubbing the butter into the flour until the mixture resembles bread crumbs. Stir in the sugar and cinnamon and spread out over a large baking sheet. Bake for 10–15 minutes until the crumble is golden brown. Leave aside to cool then break the crumble into small pieces and sprinkle two thirds of the crumble over the base of the prepared cake pan.

For the filling, soak the gelatine leaves in water until they are soft.

In a large mixing bowl, whisk together the cream cheese, ricotta and sugar until smooth.

Put the cream in a heatproof bowl set over a pan of simmering water and heat gently. Squeeze the water from the gelatine leaves and stir them into the warm cream until the gelatine has dissolved. Carefully add the gelatine cream to the cream cheese mixture, passing it through a sieve/strainer as you go to remove any gelatine pieces that have not dissolved. Beat the mixture until it is smooth and slightly thick, then stir in the plum purée. Pour the mixture over the crumble base and chill in the refrigerator for 3–4 hours or overnight until set.

To serve, place the reserved 12 plum halves on top of the cheesecake and drizzle over the reserved plum juice. Sprinkle the remaining crumble over the cheesecake to serve.

caramelized banoffee cheesecake

This cheesecake is inspired by the popular dessert, banoffee pie – toffee and banana cheesecake filling, topped with caramelized bananas. With banana chips in the base for extra crunch and flavour, if you love bananas, this is the dessert for you. Serve with extra whipped cream on the side, if you wish.

FOR THE BASE

200 g/7 oz. digestive biscuits/graham crackers

50 g/¾ cup dried banana chips

115 g/1 stick butter, melted

FOR THE FILLING

2 ripe bananas

freshly squeezed juice of 1 lemon

500 g/generous 2 cups cream cheese

500 g/generous 2 cups ricotta

4 eggs

1 teaspoon vanilla bean paste

400 g/1¾ cups caramel condensed milk or dulce de leche

2 teaspoons ground cinnamon

FOR THE TOPPING

50 g/¼ cup caster/white sugar

30 g/2 tablespoons butter

4 ripe bananas, peeled and sliced

freshly squeezed juice of ½ lemon

3 tablespoons flaked/slivered almonds

a 23-cm/9-inch round springform cake pan, greased and lined

SERVES 12

Preheat the oven to 170°C (325°F) Gas 3.

To make the crumb base, crush the biscuits/graham crackers and banana chips to fine crumbs in a food processor or place in a clean plastic bag and bash with a rolling pin. Transfer the crumbs to a mixing bowl and stir in the melted butter. Press the buttery banana crumbs into the base of the prepared cake pan firmly using the back of a spoon. Wrap the outside of the pan in cling film/plastic wrap and place in a roasting pan half full with water, ensuring that the water is not so high as to spill out. Set aside.

For the filling, blitz the bananas and lemon juice to a smooth purée in a food processor, or mash together with a fork.

In a large mixing bowl, whisk together the cream cheese and ricotta. Add the eggs, vanilla, caramel condensed milk, cinnamon and banana purée and whisk again until smooth.

Pour the banana filling mixture over the crumb base, then transfer the cheesecake, in its waterbath, to the preheated oven and bake for 1 – 1¼ hours until the cheesecake is set but still has a slight wobble in the centre. Remove the cheesecake from the waterbath and slide a knife around the edge of the pan to release the cheesecake and prevent it from cracking. Leave to cool completely in the pan, then chill in the refrigerator for at least 3 hours before serving.

Toast the almonds in a dry frying pan until golden brown, stirring all the time so that they do not burn. Transfer to a plate and leave to cool.

For the banana topping, heat the sugar and butter in a large frying pan until the sugar dissolves and caramelizes. Add the sliced bananas to the pan, tossing in the caramel until golden. Remove from the heat and squeeze over the lemon juice. Arrange the bananas on top of the cheesecake to serve and sprinkle over the toasted almonds.

bananas foster cheesecake

FOR THE BASE

2 small bananas

freshly squeezed juice of ½ lemon

55 g/¼ cup dark muscovado sugar

55 g/4 tablespoons butter, softened

1 egg

75 g/generous ½ cup self-raising flour

1 teaspoon ground cinnamon

30 g/¼ cup walnut pieces

30 g/¼ cup raisins

FOR THE FILLING

4 sheets leaf gelatine

200 g/scant 1 cup cream cheese

170 g/¾ cup mascarpone cheese

100 g/½ cup caster/white sugar

2 ripe bananas

freshly squeezed juice of 1 lemon

250 ml/1 cup double/heavy cream

2 teaspoons ground cinnamon

a few drops of yellow food colouring

FOR THE RUM SAUCE

100 g/7 tablespoons butter

100 g/½ cup caster/white sugar

1 teaspoon ground cinnamon

160 ml/⅔ cup double/heavy cream

100 ml/generous ⅓ cup dark rum

grated white chocolate, to decorate

a 23-cm/9-inch round springform cake pan, greased and lined

SERVES 10

This cheesecake is inspired by the classic banana sundae dessert, bananas foster which contains bananas and ice cream and is topped with a rum caramel sauce. Delicious! If you want to make this cheesecake a little closer to the original, you can use a tall round cutter to cut 5 circles from the cheesecake when it is set. Cut 5 cylinders of vanilla ice cream with the same cutter and insert into the holes in the cheesecake just before serving.

Preheat the oven to 180°C (350°F) Gas 4.

To make the base, blitz the bananas and lemon juice to a smooth purée in a food processor, or mash together with a fork.

In a large mixing bowl, beat together the sugar and butter until light and creamy. Add the egg and beat again. Sift in the flour, then add the banana purée, cinnamon, walnut pieces and raisins and whisk well so that everything is incorporated. Pour the mixture into the prepared cake pan and bake in the preheated oven for 15–20 minutes until the cake is golden brown and springs back when pressed gently in the centre. Leave to cool in the pan.

For the filling, soak the gelatine leaves in water until they are soft.

In a large mixing bowl, whisk together the cream cheese, mascarpone and sugar until light and creamy.

Blitz the banana with the lemon juice to a purée in a food processor, or mash together with a fork, then beat the purée into the cheesecake mixture.

Put the cream and cinnamon in a heatproof bowl set over a pan of simmering water and heat gently. Squeeze the water from the gelatine leaves and stir them into the cream until the gelatine has dissolved. Pass the cinnamon cream through a sieve/strainer to remove any undissolved gelatine pieces, then whisk into the cheese mixture. Add a few drops of yellow food colouring, and pour the cheesecake mixture over the cake base and tap the pan gently so that the cheesecake filling is level. Chill in the refrigerator for 3 hours or overnight until set.

For the rum sauce, put the butter, sugar and cinnamon in a saucepan and simmer until the sugar has dissolved. Add the cream and simmer for a further few minutes. Remove from the heat and stir in the rum, then set aside to cool.

Serve slices of the cheesecake drizzled with the rum sauce and sprinkled with the grated white chocolate.

strawberry and cream cheesecake

Some pairings are a match made in heaven – strawberries and cream is one of them. Rather than the traditional biscuit/cookie base, this cheesecake has a delicate almond sponge which pairs perfectly with the strawberries. It also makes this cheesecake gluten free. Packed with lots of fresh berries and very naughty clotted cream, this is a cheesecake for a special occasion.

FOR THE BASE

55 g/4 tablespoons butter, softened

55 g/¼ cup caster/white sugar

1 large egg

55 g/½ cup ground almonds

FOR THE FILLING

200 g/2 cups strawberries, hulled

225 g/1 cup clotted cream (if unavailable, use crème fraîche)

600 g/2⅔ cups cream cheese

120 ml/½ cup double/heavy cream

100 g/½ cup caster/white sugar

4 eggs

FOR THE TOPPING

250 ml/1 cup double/heavy cream, whipped to stiff peaks

200 g/2 cups strawberries, halved

a 23-cm/9-inch round springform cake pan, greased and lined

SERVES 12

Preheat the oven to 180°C (350°F) Gas 4.

For the base, cream together the butter and sugar in a large mixing bowl until light and creamy. Add the egg and whisk again. Fold in the ground almonds, then spoon the mixture into the prepared cake pan. Bake in the preheated oven for 10–15 minutes until golden brown, then leave the base in the pan to cool.

When you are ready to prepare the filling, preheat the oven to 170°C (325°F) Gas 3. Wrap the outside of the pan in cling film/plastic wrap and place in a roasting pan half full with water, ensuring that the water is not so high as to spill out. Set aside.

For the filling, blitz the strawberries, clotted cream, cream cheese, cream, sugar and eggs in a blender until smooth. Pour the strawberry cream over the sponge base, then transfer the cheesecake, in its waterbath, to the preheated oven and bake for 50–60 minutes until the cheesecake is set but still wobbles slightly in the centre. Remove the cheesecake from the waterbath and slide a knife around the edge of the pan to release the cheesecake and prevent it from cracking. Leave to cool completely in the pan, then chill in the refrigerator for at least 3 hours before serving.

When you are ready to serve, remove the cheesecake from the pan and place on a serving plate. Spread the whipped cream over the top of the cheesecake, then arrange the strawberries over the cream. Serve straight away or chill in the refrigerator until ready to serve.

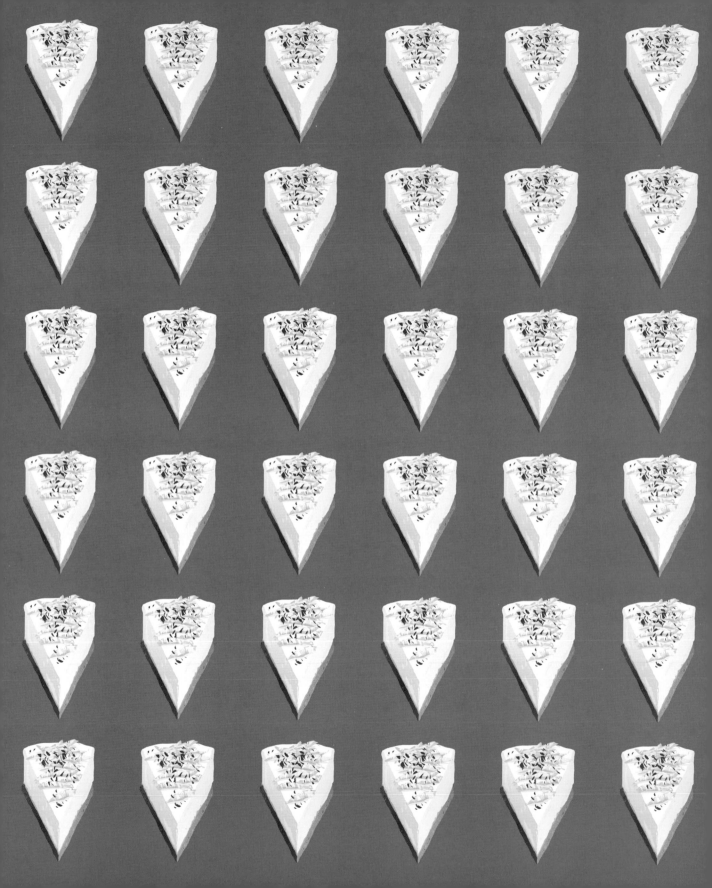

candy bar cheesecakes

FOR THE CRUMB BASE

250 g/9 oz. digestive biscuits/graham crackers

50 g/generous ⅓ cup salted peanuts

100 g/7 tablespoons butter, melted

FOR THE FILLING

450 g/2 cups quark/farmer cheese

600 g/2⅔ cups cream cheese

250 ml/1 cup double/heavy cream

4 eggs

100 g/½ cup caster/white sugar

3 tablespoons crunchy peanut butter

200 g/1¼ cups milk chocolate chips

FOR THE BRITTLE

200 g/1 cup caster/white sugar

80 ml/⅓ cup golden/light corn syrup

150 g/1 generous cup salted peanuts

2 tablespoons crunchy peanut butter

1 teaspoon vanilla bean paste

50 g/3½ tablespoons salted butter

1 scant teaspoon bicarbonate of soda/baking soda

FOR THE TOPPING

250 ml/1 cup double/heavy cream

50 g/2 oz. dark chocolate, melted

a 23-cm/9-inch round springform cake pan, greased and lined

a sugar thermometer

a silicone mat or greased baking sheet

a piping bag fitted with a large star nozzle/tip

SERVES 12

peanut brittle cheesecake

Making your own peanut brittle is quick and easy to do and is definitely worth the effort. The recipe makes more brittle than is needed, but it stores well in an airtight container and it's a good idea to make extra as it's the bit that everyone loves best! This cheesecake is rich so you only need to serve thin slices.

Preheat the oven to 170°C (325°F) Gas 3.

To make the crumb base, crush the biscuits/graham crackers and peanuts to fine crumbs in a food processor or place in a clean plastic bag and bash with a rolling pin. Transfer the crumbs to a mixing bowl and stir in the melted butter. Press the buttery crumbs into the base of the prepared cake pan firmly using the back of a spoon. Wrap the outside of the pan in cling film/plastic wrap and place in a roasting pan half full with water, ensuring that the water is not so high as to spill out. Set aside.

For the filling, whisk together the quark, cream cheese, cream, eggs, sugar and peanut butter in a large mixing bowl until smooth. Stir in the chocolate chips and spoon the mixture over the base in the pan. Carefully transfer the cheesecake, in its waterbath, to the preheated oven and bake for 1–1¼ hours until the cheesecake is golden brown on top and still wobbles slightly in the centre. Leave to cool completely in the pan then chill in the refrigerator for 3 hours or overnight for best results.

For the brittle, heat the sugar, syrup and 40 ml/3 tablespoons water in a saucepan until the sugar has melted, then bring to the boil until the temperature reaches 122°C (252°F) or hard ball stage. (A sugar thermometer is best for this, but if you do not have one, boil the sugar for about 5 minutes then carefully drop a small amount of the liquid into cold water. If the mixture forms into a ball that is solid when you remove it from the water, the mixture is ready.) Add the peanuts, peanut butter, vanilla paste and butter to the pan and beat well – the mixture will become stiff. Beat in the bicarbonate of soda/baking soda, then tip the mixture onto the silicone mat or greased baking sheet, taking care as it will be very hot. Spread the mixture out into a layer about 1cm/½ inch thick and leave to cool. When the brittle is cold, break it into small pieces using your hands or a rolling pin.

To assemble, remove the cheesecake from the pan. Whip the cream to stiff peaks then spoon into the piping bag. Pipe small stars in a ring around the outside edge of the cheesecake. Repeat with two more rings, leaving a gap in the middle. Sprinkle over some of the peanut brittle and, using a fork or spoon, drizzle with the melted chocolate in thin lines to decorate. Store in the refrigerator until you are ready to serve.

rocky road cheesecake

This decadent cheesecake is the ultimate chocoholic's indulgence. It has a classic rocky road topping with marshmallows, nuts and cherries, all nestling on a creamy chocolate filling, studded with fudge pieces. This cheesecake is rich so is best served in thin slices!

FOR THE CRUMB CASE

300 g/10½ oz. Oreo cookies

150 g/1¼ sticks butter, melted

FOR THE FILLING

6 sheets leaf gelatine

320 g/generous 1⅓ cups chocolate cream cheese

250 g/generous 1 cup mascarpone cheese

1 teaspoon vanilla bean paste

100 g/½ cup caster/white sugar

400 ml/1¾ cups double/heavy cream

100 g/3½ oz. mini fudge pieces

FOR THE TOPPING

80 g/⅔ cup honey-roasted cashews

100 g/¾ cup glacé/candied cherries, halved

40 g/1 cup mini marshmallows

100 g/3½ oz. chocolate-coated honeycomb balls (such as Maltesers)

100 g/3½ oz. dark chocolate

a 23-cm/9-inch round springform cake pan, greased and lined

SERVES 12

To make the crumb case, crush the Oreo cookies to fine crumbs in a food processor or place in a clean plastic bag and bash with a rolling pin. Transfer the crumbs to a mixing bowl and stir in the melted butter. Press the buttery crumbs into the base and sides of the prepared cake pan firmly using the back of a spoon. You need the crumbs to come up about 3–4 cm/1½ inches high on the side of the pan so that they make a case for the filling.

For the filling, soak the gelatine leaves in water until they are soft.

In a large mixing bowl, whisk together the chocolate cream cheese, mascarpone, vanilla and sugar until smooth.

Put the cream in a heatproof bowl set over a pan of simmering water and warm gently. Squeeze the water from the gelatine leaves and stir them into the cream until the gelatine has dissolved. Pass the cream through a sieve/strainer to remove any undissolved gelatine pieces, then add to the cheese mixture. Beat until the mixture is smooth and slightly thick, then stir in the fudge pieces. Pour the mixture over the crumb case and chill in the refrigerator for 3–4 hours or overnight until set.

When set, sprinkle the cashews, cherries, marshmallows and chocolate honeycomb balls over the top of the cheesecake. Melt the dark chocolate in a heatproof bowl set over a pan of simmering water and drizzle it over the rocky road topping. Chill in the refrigerator to set before serving.

honeycomb cheesecake

FOR THE HONEYCOMB

200 g/1 cup golden caster/natural raw cane sugar

3 tablespoons runny honey

1 teaspoon vanilla bean paste

¼ teaspoon cream of tartar

30 g/2 tablespoons butter

a pinch of salt

1 teaspoon bicarbonate of soda/baking soda

FOR THE CRUMB BASE

200 g/7 oz. digestive biscuits/graham crackers

100 g/7 tablespoons butter, melted

FOR THE FILLING

600 g/2⅔ cups cream cheese

300 ml/1¼ cups sour cream

160 ml/⅔ cup double/heavy cream

120 ml/½ cup runny honey

4 eggs, plus 1 egg white

1 teaspoon vanilla bean paste

1 tablespoon runny honey, to serve

a sugar thermometer (optional)

a silicone mat or greased baking sheet

a 23-cm/9-inch round springform cake pan, greased and lined

SERVES 12

Honeycomb, sponge candy or cinder toffee – however you call this delicious sweet treat, it is loved by all. Coating it in beaten egg white prevents it melting in contact with liquid and gives this cheesecake delicious pockets of honeycomb-flavoured caramel.

Begin by preparing the honeycomb. Put the sugar, honey, vanilla, cream of tartar, butter, salt and 60 ml/¼ cup water in a large heavy-based saucepan (the mixture will triple in size when you add the bicarbonate of soda/baking soda, so make sure the pan is large enough for this). Simmer until the sugar and butter dissolve, then heat to 122°C (252°F), hard ball stage, taking care that the caramel does not burn. (A sugar thermometer is best for this, but if you do not have one, boil the sugar for about 5 minutes then carefully drop a small amount of the liquid into cold water. If the mixture forms into a ball that is solid when you remove it from the water, the mixture is ready.) Remove the caramel from the heat and beat in the bicarbonate of soda/baking soda. Tip out immediately onto the silicone mat or baking sheet and leave to cool. When cool, break the honeycomb into small pieces using a rolling pin. Store half in an airtight container and keep the remainder out to add to the cheesecake.

Preheat the oven to 170°C (325°F) Gas 3.

To make the crumb base, crush the biscuits/graham crackers to fine crumbs in a food processor or place in a clean plastic bag and bash with a rolling pin. Transfer the crumbs to a mixing bowl and stir in the melted butter. Press the buttery crumbs into the base of the prepared cake pan firmly using the back of a spoon. Wrap the outside of the pan in cling film/plastic wrap and place in a roasting pan half full with water, ensuring that the water is not so high as to spill out. Set aside.

For the filling, whisk together the cream cheese, sour cream, double/heavy cream, honey, whole eggs and vanilla in a large mixing bowl. In a separate bowl, whisk the egg white until foamy, then stir in the honeycomb pieces and toss to coat them in the egg. Stir the honeycomb pieces into the filling mixture (you do not need to add the excess egg white), then pour the mixture over the crumb base. Transfer the cheesecake, in its water bath, to the preheated oven. Bake for 45–60 minutes until the cheesecake is set but still wobbles slightly in the centre. The top will appear dark where the honeycomb has caramelized in the heat. Remove the cheesecake from the waterbath and leave to cool, then chill in the fridge for at least 3 hours.

When you are ready to serve, heat the honey gently in a saucepan, then brush it over the top of the cheesecake with a pastry brush and sprinkle with the reserved honeycomb.

chocolate hazelnut cheesecake

My friend Maren loves Nutella so I developed this cheesecake recipe for her. She managed two slices which, given how rich this cheesecake is, is nothing short of a miracle! It is bursting with Ferrero Rocher chocolates and a chocolate chip hazelnut base. If you love Nutella then I can't urge you enough to try this cheesecake!

FOR THE CRUMB BASE

230 g/8 oz. hazelnut choc chip cookies

50 g/⅓ cup plus 1 tablespoon toasted hazelnut pieces

100 g/7 tablespoons butter, melted

FOR THE FILLING

6 sheets leaf gelatine

300 g/1⅓ cups cream cheese

250 g/generous 1 cup ricotta

200 g/generous ¾ cup chocolate hazelnut spread (such as Nutella), at room temperature

250 ml/1 cup double/heavy cream

100 g/3½ oz. dark chocolate, chopped

10 Ferrero Rocher chocolates, quartered

FOR THE TOPPING

50 g/2 oz. dark chocolate, melted

3 generous tablespoons chopped roasted hazelnuts

150 ml/⅔ cup double/heavy cream, whipped

6 Ferrero Rocher chocolates

a 23-cm/9-inch round springform cake pan, greased and lined

a piping bag fitted with a large star nozzle/tip

SERVES 12

For the crumb base, crush the cookies to fine crumbs in a food processor or place in a clean plastic bag and bash with a rolling pin. Transfer the crumbs to a mixing bowl and stir in the hazelnuts and melted butter. Press the buttery crumbs into the base of the prepared cake pan firmly using the back of a spoon.

For the filling, soak the gelatine leaves in water until they are soft.

In a large mixing bowl, whisk together the cream cheese, ricotta and chocolate hazelnut spread until light and creamy.

Put the cream in a heatproof bowl set over a pan of simmering water and heat gently. Squeeze the water from the gelatine leaves and stir them into the warm cream until the gelatine has dissolved. Add the chocolate and stir until melted.

Carefully add the chocolate cream to the cream cheese mixture, passing it through a sieve/strainer to remove any undissolved gelatine pieces. Beat until the mixture is smooth and slightly thick, then stir in the chopped Ferrero Rocher pieces. Pour the mixture over the crumb base and chill in the refrigerator for 3–4 hours or overnight until set.

To serve, drizzle half of the melted chocolate in fine lines over the top of the cheesecake using a fork. Sprinkle the centre of the cheesecake with the hazelnuts and drizzle the remaining chocolate in fine lines over the nuts. Spoon the cream into the piping bag and pipe 12 large stars of cream around the edge of the cheesecake. Cut each Ferrero Rocher in half using a sharp knife and place one on top of each cream star. Store in the refrigerator until you are ready to serve.

brownie cheesecake

Brownies and cheesecake are two of my favourite sweet treats and putting them together in this recipe makes one of my favourite cheesecakes. The cheesecake is perfect to serve for afternoon tea or morning coffee but also makes an indulgent dessert served with scoops of vanilla ice cream and hot chocolate sauce. As with all brownie recipes, feel free to add additional ingredients – omit the nuts if you wish, and add chocolate chips and orange zest for the perfect chocolate orange treat.

FOR THE BROWNIES

100 g/7 tablespoons butter

150 g/5½ oz. dark chocolate

100 g/½ cup caster/white sugar

100 g/½ cup soft dark brown sugar

2 eggs

1 teaspoon vanilla extract

80 g/scant ⅔ cup plain/all-purpose flour, sifted

50 g/½ cup chopped pecans

FOR THE TOPPING

150 g/⅔ cup cream cheese

160 ml/⅔ cup sour cream

50 g/¼ cup caster/white sugar

1 teaspoon vanilla bean paste

2 eggs

30 g/scant ¼ cup plain/all-purpose flour, sifted

125 g/4½ oz. dark chocolate, chopped

a 23-cm/9-inch round springform cake pan, greased and lined

SERVES 12

Preheat the oven to 180°C (350°F) Gas 4.

To prepare the brownies, melt the butter and chocolate in a heatproof bowl set over a small pan of simmering water, taking care that the bottom of the bowl does not touch the water. Stir until melted, then leave to cool.

In a large mixing bowl, whisk together the sugars and eggs with the vanilla until doubled in size and the mixture is very light and creamy. Slowly pour in the cooled melted chocolate mixture, whisking all the time. Fold in the flour and nuts, then pour into the prepared cake pan.

For the cheesecake topping, whisk together the cream cheese, sour cream, sugar, vanilla, eggs and flour until smooth, then stir through the chopped chocolate. Place large spoonfuls of the cheesecake mixture at intervals on top of the brownie mixture. Swirl the cheesecake and brownie mixtures together with a round-bladed knife to create swirled patterns.

Bake the cheesecake in the preheated oven for 40–45 minutes until a crust has formed on the brownie and the cheesecake mixture is set. Allow to cool before serving.

sticky toffee pudding cheesecake

I don't know anyone who doesn't love sticky toffee pudding. It is one of those desserts that when you see it listed on a menu, you know you have no choice but to order it. This is my cheesecake version with a cake base inspired by the classic toffee pudding and a rich caramel sauce to serve poured over each slice.

FOR THE CAKE BASE

60 g/4 tablespoons butter, softened

60 g/⅓ cup muscovado sugar

1 egg

60 g/scant ½ cup self-raising flour

1 generous tablespoon crème fraîche

40 g/⅓ cup finely chopped pecan nuts

40 g/¼ cup finely chopped dates

FOR THE FILLING

600 ml/2½ cups crème fraîche

600 g/2⅔ cups cream cheese

4 eggs

400 g/1¾ cups caramel condensed milk or dulce de leche

FOR THE TOFFEE SAUCE

80 g/scant ½ cup caster/white sugar

40 g/3¼ tablespoons muscovado sugar

50 g/3½ tablespoons butter

a pinch of salt

250 ml/1 cup double/heavy cream

clotted cream or crème fraîche, to serve

a 23-cm/9-inch round springform cake pan, greased and lined

SERVES 12

Preheat the oven to 180°C (350°F) Gas 4.

For the base, whisk together the butter and sugar in a large mixing bowl until creamy. Add the egg and beat again. Sift in the flour and add the crème fraîche, pecan nuts and dates. Spoon the mixture into the prepared cake pan and bake for 15–20 minutes until the cake is golden brown and springs back when pressed gently in the centre. Leave to cool in the pan. Turn the oven temperature down to 170°C (325°F) Gas 3.

When the base is cool, wrap the outside of the pan in cling film/plastic wrap and place in a roasting pan half full with water, ensuring that the water is not so high as to spill out. Set aside.

For the filling, whisk together the crème fraîche, cream cheese, eggs and caramel condensed milk. Pour the mixture on top of the cake base and transfer the cheesecake, in its waterbath, to the preheated oven. Bake for 1–1¼ hours until golden brown on top and still with a slight wobble in the centre. Remove the cheesecake from the waterbath and slide a knife around the edge of the pan to release the cheesecake and prevent it from cracking. Leave to cool, then transfer to the refrigerator to chill for at least 3 hours or preferably overnight.

For the toffee sauce, put the sugars, butter, salt and 200 ml/¾ cup of the cream in a heavy-based saucepan set over a gentle heat and simmer until the sugar has dissolved and you have a thick toffee sauce. Remove from the heat and add the remaining 50 ml/¼ cup cream. Leave to cool then serve with the cheesecake, along with clotted cream or crème fraîche.

toffee pecan cheesecake

You really can't beat a classic pecan pie topped with a buttery caramel and filled with glistening nuts. There is no biscuit base in this cheesecake – instead the pan is lined with finely chopped pecans for a nutty crust, which means that this cheesecake is perfectly gluten free.

FOR THE NUT CRUST

30 g/2 tablespoons butter, softened

100 g/1 cup finely chopped pecans

FOR THE FILLING

600 g/2⅔ cups cream cheese

500 g/generous 2 cups ricotta

4 large eggs

250 ml/1 cup maple syrup

FOR THE TOPPING

75 g/generous ⅓ cup caster/white sugar

75 g/packed ⅓ cup dark brown sugar

3 tablespoons golden/light corn syrup

1 generous teaspoon ground cinnamon

1 teaspoon vanilla bean paste

40 g/3 tablespoons butter

1 egg, plus 1 egg yolk, beaten

100 g/generous ¾ cup pecan halves

a 26-cm/10-inch round springform cake pan, greased and lined

SERVES 12

Preheat the oven to 170°C (325°F) Gas 3.

To prepare the pan, spread the softened butter around the sides and base of the pan. Sprinkle the chopped pecan nuts into the pan and shake the pan so that the base and sides are covered with pecan pieces.

In a large mixing bowl, whisk together the cream cheese and ricotta, then add the eggs and maple syrup and whisk until the mixture is smooth. Spoon the mixture into the prepared pan, set the pan on a large baking sheet and bake in the preheated oven for 45–60 minutes. The cheesecake is cooked when it is golden brown on top and the centre still has a very slight wobble. Slide a knife around the edge of the pan to release the cheesecake and prevent it from cracking, then leave to cool.

To prepare the caramel glaze for the topping, heat the sugars, syrup, cinnamon, vanilla paste and butter in a saucepan until the sugars have dissolved and the mixture is syrupy. Remove from the heat and let cool for 10 minutes, then whisk in the beaten egg and yolk. Pass the mixture through a sieve/strainer to remove any impurities.

Arrange the pecan halves in a ring around the edge of the cheesecake whilst still in the pan, then spoon over some of the caramel glaze. You may not need all of the glaze but any extra can be served alongside the cheesecake to drizzle over. Chill the cheesecake in the refrigerator overnight for best results and remove from the pan just before serving.

peppermint bark cheesecake

My friend Martha Murphy lives in the most quintessential American house that I have ever visited – beautiful weather boarding and a perfect white picket fence and it was in her kitchen that she taught me to make peppermint bark. For those of you unfamiliar with this delicious winter treat, quite simply it is peppermint-flavoured white chocolate sprinkled with crushed candy canes. I love it! This cheesecake makes a lovely Christmas dessert and is perfect for using up any candy canes left on your Christmas tree.

FOR THE CRUMB BASE

180 g/6 oz. chocolate oat biscuits/cookies (such as Hobnobs)

60 g/4 tablespoons butter, melted

FOR THE FILLING

100 g/3½ oz. white chocolate

250 g/generous 1 cup mascarpone cheese

250 ml/1 cup crème fraîche

1 teaspoon peppermint extract

1 teaspoon vanilla extract

FOR THE PEPPERMINT BARK

150 g/5½ oz. white chocolate

1 teaspoon peppermint extract

5 peppermint candy canes

white edible glitter (optional)

a 20-cm/8-inch loose-based cake pan, greased and lined

a silicone mat (optional)

SERVES 10

To make the base, crush the biscuits/cookies to fine crumbs in a food processor or place in a clean plastic bag and bash with a rolling pin. Transfer the crumbs to a mixing bowl and stir in the melted butter. Press the buttery crumbs into the base of the prepared cake pan firmly using the back of a spoon.

For the filling, melt the white chocolate in a heatproof bowl set over a pan of simmering water. Remove the bowl from the heat and leave the chocolate to cool, but not set.

In a large mixing bowl, whisk together the mascarpone and crème fraîche in a large mixing bowl. Stir through the cooled white chocolate and the peppermint and vanilla extracts. It is important that the white chocolate is cool when it is added to the mixture otherwise it will set in small pieces in the cream. Spoon the mixture over the crumb base and level with a spatula. Chill in the refrigerator for at least 3 hours.

For the peppermint bark, melt the chocolate in a heatproof bowl set over a pan of simmering water. Remove from the heat and stir in the peppermint extract, then spread out in a thin layer on a silicone mat or sheet of greaseproof/waxed paper. Crush the peppermint candy canes into small pieces in a clean plastic bag using a rolling pin, then sprinkle the red and white candy pieces over the white chocolate and leave to set in the refrigerator.

When ready to serve, remove the cheesecake from the pan and place it on a serving plate. Break the peppermint bark into small shards using a sharp knife and decorate the top of the cheesecake with them. Sprinkle with edible glitter, if using, to serve.

chocolate toffee crunch cheesecake

The day my favourite lunch café stopped serving Daim Bar cheesecakes was a very sad one indeed. It was my favourite treat at the time and I was bereft. Daim Bar (similar to a US Heath bar), originally from Sweden, is a candy bar like no other – with brittle almond caramel and chocolate. It is the perfect addition to a cheesecake.

FOR THE CRUMB BASE

250 g/9 oz. caramelized biscuits/cookies (such as Lotus)

125 g/1 stick plus 1 tablespoon butter, melted

FOR THE FILLING

400 g/1¾ cups cream cheese

250 g/generous 1 cup ricotta

225 g/1 cup clotted cream (if unavailable, use crème fraîche)

400 g/1¾ cups condensed milk

finely grated zest of 1 lemon

4 eggs

180 g/6 oz. chopped Daim/Heath bar

a 23-cm/9-inch round springform cake pan, greased and lined

SERVES 12

Preheat the oven to 170°C (325°F) Gas 3.

To make the crumb base, crush the biscuits/cookies to fine crumbs in a food processor or place in a clean plastic bag and bash with a rolling pin. Transfer the crumbs to a mixing bowl and stir in the melted butter. Press the buttery crumbs into the base of the prepared cake pan firmly using the back of a spoon.

For the filling, whisk together the cream cheese, ricotta and clotted cream in a large mixing bowl. Add the condensed milk, lemon zest and eggs and whisk again until smooth. Stir in two thirds of the Daim/Heath bars so that they are evenly distributed, then pour the mixture over the crumb base.

Bake the cheesecake in the preheated oven for 10 minutes, then carefully sprinkle the remaining chopped Daim/Heath bars over the top of the cheesecake. A slight skin will have formed on top of the cheesecake which will hold the Daim/Heath bar pieces on top of the cheesecake. Bake for a further 40–50 minutes until the cheesecake is set but still wobbles slightly in the centre. Leave to cool completely then chill for at least 3 hours in the refrigerator before serving.

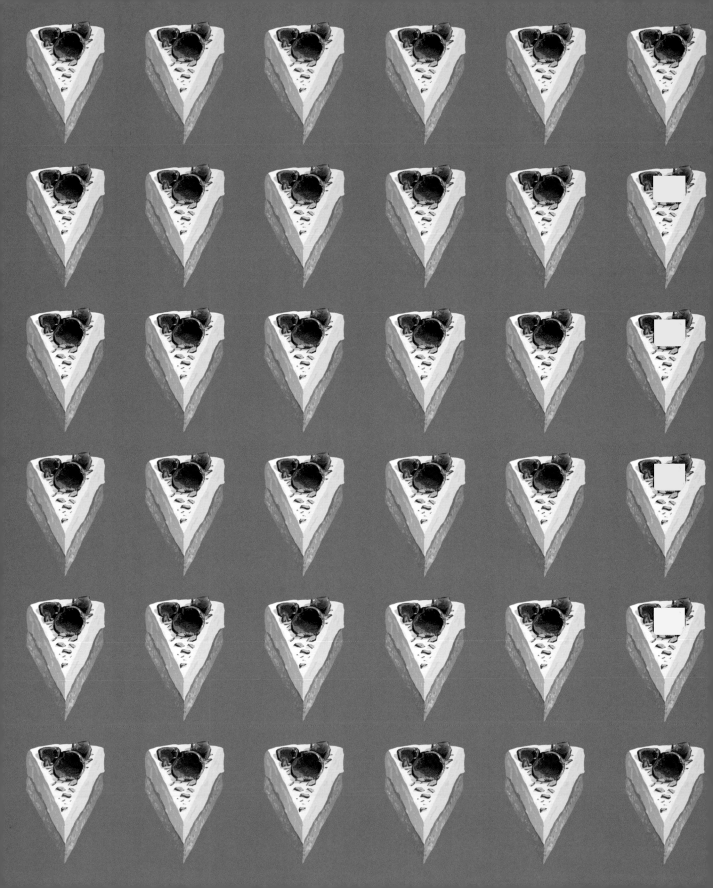

gourmet cheesecakes

chocolate chilli cheesecake

Chilli may sound a strange accompaniment to chocolate but it really does enhance the flavour of the cocoa and adds a warming heat. Bars of chilli-flavoured chocolate are available in most supermarkets, but if you cannot find any use dark chocolate and add a little chilli powder. Candying the chilli takes away some of the heat and makes a great looking fiery decoration, but if you are less brave use red sugar sprinkles instead.

FOR THE DECORATION

8 bird's eye chillies

100 g/½ cup caster/white sugar

FOR THE CRUMB BASE

250 g/9 oz. chocolate digestive biscuits/graham crackers

100 g/7 tablespoons butter, melted

FOR THE FILLING

6 sheets leaf gelatine

300 g/1⅓ cups cream cheese

250 g/generous 1 cup mascarpone cheese

100 g/½ cup caster/white sugar

400 ml/1¾ cups double/heavy cream

100 g/3½ oz. dark chilli chocolate, melted

FOR THE TOPPING

100 g/3½ oz. dark chilli chocolate

60 ml/¼ cup double/heavy cream

20 g/1½ tablespoons butter

60 ml/¼ cup golden/light corn syrup

8 x 6-cm/2½-inch diameter chef's rings
(6 cm/2½ inches deep), greased

MAKES 8

Begin by preparing the chillies. Put them in a saucepan with the sugar and 250 ml/1 cup water and simmer for 15 minutes until the chillies are soft and the liquid is syrupy. Set aside to cool in the syrup.

To make the crumb bases, crush the biscuits/graham crackers to fine crumbs in a food processor or place in a clean plastic bag and bash with a rolling pin. Transfer the crumbs to a mixing bowl and stir in the melted butter. Place the chef's rings on a baking sheet and divide the buttery crumbs between them, pressing down firmly with the back of a spoon.

For the filling, soak the gelatine leaves in water until they are soft.

In a large mixing bowl, whisk together the cream cheese, mascarpone and sugar until light and creamy.

Put the cream in a heatproof bowl set over a saucepan of simmering water, and heat gently. Squeeze the water out of the gelatine leaves and stir them into the warm cream until the gelatine has dissolved. Pass through a sieve/strainer to remove any undissolved gelatine pieces, then stir in the melted chilli chocolate. Carefully add the chocolate cream to the cream cheese mixture and beat until everything is incorporated. Pour the mixture over the crumb bases in the chef's rings.

For the ganache topping, put the chocolate, cream and butter in a heatproof bowl set over a pan of simmering water and stir until the chocolate and butter have melted. Add the syrup and stir again until glossy. Remove from the heat and leave to cool for a few minutes then gently spread over the top of the cheesecakes. Chill in the refrigerator for 3 hours or overnight until the cheesecakes are set. To serve, remove the cheesecakes from the chef's rings and top each with a candied chilli (discarding the sugar syrup).

chocolate ginger cheesecake

Chocolate and ginger make an indulgent combination and this cheesecake is no exception. Decorated with pretty swirled chocolate patterns and bursting with tiny pieces of stem ginger, this is one of my favourite recipes in this book.

FOR THE CRUMB CASE

300 g/10½ oz. ginger biscuits/cookies

150 g/1¼ sticks butter, melted

FOR THE FILLING

650 g/2¾–3 cups cream cheese

600 ml/2½ cups crème fraîche

4 eggs

100 g/½ cup caster/white sugar

200 g/7 oz. dark chocolate, melted and cooled

6 balls preserved stem ginger, finely chopped

1 tablespoon ginger syrup (from the preserved stem ginger jar)

150 g/5½ oz. dark chocolate, chopped

2 tablespoons plain/all-purpose flour, sifted

FOR THE TOPPING

150 g/5½ oz. white chocolate

30 g/1 oz. dark chocolate

a 23-cm/9-inch round springform cake pan, greased and lined

a piping bag fitted with a small round nozzle/tip (optional)

SERVES 12

Preheat the oven to 170°C (325°F) Gas 3.

To make the crumb case, crush the biscuits/cookies to fine crumbs in a food processor or place in a clean plastic bag and bash with a rolling pin. Transfer the crumbs to a mixing bowl and stir in the melted butter. Press the buttery crumbs into the base and sides of the prepared cake pan firmly using the back of a spoon. You need the crumbs to come up about 3–4 cm/1½ inches high on the side of the pan so that they make a case for the filling. Wrap the outside of the pan in cling film/plastic wrap and place in a roasting pan half full with water, ensuring that the water is not so high as to spill out. Set aside.

For the filling, whisk together the cream cheese, crème fraîche, eggs, sugar, melted chocolate, finely chopped ginger, syrup and chopped chocolate in a large mixing bowl. Sift the flour over the mixture and stir in, then pour the mixture into the crumb case. Bake in the preheated oven for 1–1¼ hours until set but still with a slight wobble in the centre. Turn off the heat and leave to cool completely in the oven, then transfer to the refrigerator to chill for at least 3 hours or preferably overnight.

Once chilled, melt the white and dark chocolate for the decoration in separate heatproof bowls set over 2 pans of simmering water. Leave to cool slightly, then spread the white chocolate in a thin layer over the top of the cheesecake. Spoon the dark chocolate into the piping bag and pipe swirls over the top of the cheesecake in pretty patterns. If you do not have a piping bag, you can swirl patterns of the chocolate using a spoon. Chill in the refrigerator until the chocolate has set before serving.

hibiscus, raspberry and pomegranate cheesecake

Elegant hibiscus flowers taste of raspberries and rhubarb and make an elaborate looking decoration on top of this cheesecake, alongside pomegranate seeds and caramel sugar swirls. The flowers are sold in jars with hibiscus syrup to preserve them and it is this syrup that is used to flavour the cheesecake. Serve with hibiscus champagne to really wow your guests!

FOR THE CRUMB BASE

200 g/7 oz. digestive biscuits/graham crackers

100 g/7 tablespoons butter, melted

150 g/generous 1 cup raspberries

50 g/⅓ cup white chocolate chips

FOR THE FILLING

6 sheets leaf gelatine

300 g/1⅓ cups cream cheese

250 g/generous 1 cup ricotta

100 g/½ cup caster/white sugar

150 ml/⅔ cup sour cream

100 ml/generous ⅓ cup hibiscus syrup

2 tablespoons rose liqueur or syrup

FOR THE TOPPING

80 g/scant ½ cup caster/white sugar

12 hibiscus flowers

pomegranate seeds

a 23-cm/9-inch round springform cake pan, greased and lined

a silicone mat (optional)

SERVES 12

For the base, crush the biscuits/graham crackers to fine crumbs in a food processor or place in a clean plastic bag and bash with a rolling pin. Transfer the crumbs to a mixing bowl and stir in the melted butter. Press the buttery crumbs into the base of the prepared cake pan firmly using the back of a spoon. Sprinkle the raspberries and chocolate chips over the base of the cheesecake.

For the filling, soak the gelatine leaves in water until they are soft.

In a large mixing bowl, whisk together the cream cheese, ricotta, sugar and sour cream until light and creamy.

Put the hibiscus syrup and rose liqueur in a heatproof bowl resting over a pan of simmering water and heat gently. Squeeze the water from the gelatine leaves and stir them into the warm syrup until the gelatine has dissolved. Carefully add the gelatine liquid to the cream cheese mixture, passing it through a sieve/strainer to remove any gelatine pieces that have not dissolved. Beat until the mixture is smooth and slightly thick, then pour over the base and chill in the refrigerator for 3–4 hours or overnight until set.

For the topping, put the sugar in a heavy-based saucepan and heat until the sugar melts and starts to caramelize. (Watch the sugar carefully as it will easily burn as it heats up.) Do not stir, but gently swirl the caramel by shaking the pan. When the caramel is golden brown, remove from the heat and leave to stand for a minute or so until the caramel just starts to thicken. Using a fork drizzle spirals and zigzags of the caramel onto the silicone mat or a sheet of greaseproof/waxed paper to make pretty decorations. Leave to cool, then store in an airtight container until needed. The caramel will become sticky if exposed to the air, so it is best to make these only an hour or so before you wish to serve the cheesecake.

When you are ready to serve, arrange the hibiscus flowers in a ring on top of the cheesecake and sprinkle over the pomegranate seeds. Decorate with the sugar decorations and serve immediately

salty honey cheesecake

In Brooklyn, New York, there is a café called Four and Twenty Blackbirds. Just the name is enough to make it a 'must visit' destination in my book. All they serve is pie – every type of pie you can imagine! Their pièce de résistance is a salty honey pie, which I have to confess being somewhat addicted to. So, in homage to a truly remarkable place, this cheesecake is my take on the salty honey pie. I still recommend a visit, but if you can't get there, this cheesecake tribute is the next best thing. You definitely need a sweet tooth for all the honey used here!

FOR THE CRUMB BASE

250 g/9 oz. caramelized biscuits/cookies (such as Lotus)

125 g/1 stick plus 1 tablespoon butter, melted

FOR THE CHEESECAKE

125 g/1 stick plus 1 tablespoon butter, melted

170 g/generous ¾ cup caster/white sugar

½ teaspoon sea salt flakes

300 g/1 cup honey

1 teaspoon vanilla bean paste

2 teaspoons white wine vinegar

300 g/1⅓ cups cream cheese

250 ml/1 cup double/heavy cream

4 eggs

a 23-cm/9-inch round springform cake pan, greased and lined

SERVES 12

Preheat the oven to 170°C (325°F) Gas 3.

To make the crumb base, crush the caramelized biscuits/cookies to fine crumbs in a food processor or place in a clean plastic bag and bash with a rolling pin. Transfer the crumbs to a mixing bowl and stir in the melted butter. Press the buttery crumbs into the base of the prepared cake pan firmly using the back of a spoon.

For the filling, whisk together the melted butter, sugar, salt flakes, honey, vanilla, vinegar and cream cheese in a large mixing bowl until smooth. Add the cream, then beat in the eggs one at a time, whisking between each addition. Pour the mixture over the crumb base and bake in the preheated oven for 45 minutes. Reduce the oven temperature to 150°C (300°F) Gas 2 and bake for about 15 minutes more until the cheesecake is set but still has a slight wobble in the centre. Turn off the heat and leave the cheesecake to cool completely in the oven, then transfer to the refrigerator to chill for at least 3 hours or overnight before serving.

florentine cheesecakes

Dainty almond florentines always remind me of Christmas, although they are delicious at any time of year. The combination of nuts, candied fruit, sugar and chocolate work perfectly in this cheesecake recipe, with a florentine base and florentines on top of each mini cheesecake. You can add other ingredients to the florentine recipe – such as a few spoonfuls of pistachios, dried apricot pieces or chopped preserved stem ginger – if you wish.

FOR THE FLORENTINES

15 glacé/candied cherries

80 g/1 cup flaked/slivered almonds

100 g/¾ cup golden or flame raisins

30 g/¼ cup plain/all-purpose flour

80 ml/⅓ cup condensed milk

2 tablespoons melted butter

1 teaspoon ground cinnamon

1 teaspoon vanilla bean paste

FOR THE FILLING

250 g/generous 1 cup cream cheese

250 g/generous 1 cup ricotta

200 g/scant 1 cup condensed milk

2 eggs

80 g/3 oz. dark chocolate, melted, to serve

2 large baking sheets, greased and lined

a 12-hole mini cheesecake or muffin pan, greased

MAKES 12

Preheat the oven to 170°C (325°F) Gas 3.

Begin by preparing the florentines. Chop the cherries into quarters, then put them in a bowl with the almonds and raisins. Sift in the flour and stir in the condensed milk, butter, cinnamon and vanilla. Place 24 small flat rounds of the mixture (about the size of your cheesecake pan holes) onto the prepared baking sheets and bake in the preheated oven for 8–12 minutes until lightly golden brown. Leave the florentines on the baking sheets to cool and leave the oven on to bake the cheesecakes, if you are preparing them straight away.

For the filling, whisk together the cream cheese, ricotta and condensed milk in a large mixing bowl, then whisk in the eggs one at a time.

Reserve the 12 neatest florentines for the tops of the cheesecakes. Place one of the remaining florentines in the base of each hole of the cheesecake pan. If the florentines are too large, break them into smaller pieces and press a few into each hole. Spoon the filling mixture into the 12 holes of the pan until they are almost full. (Depending on the size of your pan you may not need all of the mixture.) Bake the cheesecakes in the preheated oven for 20–25 minutes until they are golden brown and still wobble slightly in the centre. Remove from the oven and leave to cool.

When cool, remove the cheesecakes from the pan, releasing the sides of the cheesecake using a round-bladed knife. Spread a little melted chocolate over the top of each cheesecake and top with a florentine. Drizzle any remaining chocolate over the tops in thin lines, then chill in the refrigerator until you are ready to serve.

pine nut cheesecake

When I have served this cheesecake to friends in the past, it has provoked quite a bit of discussion. Some loved it just as the recipe below and some wanted it a bit sweeter. I like the freshness that this cheesecake has without being overly sweet, but if you like really sweet desserts then increase the amount of honey in the filling. The pine nuts on top and in the base give this cheesecake a really lovely crunch.

FOR THE CRUMB BASE

200 g/7 oz. digestive biscuits/
graham crackers

100 g/7 tablespoons butter, melted

100 g/¾ cup pine nuts

FOR THE FILLING

600 g/2⅔ cups cream cheese

600 ml/2½ cups crème fraîche

freshly squeezed juice and grated zest
of 2 lemons and 1 lime

60 ml/¼ cup runny honey
(or more to taste)

50 g/¼ cup caster/white sugar

4 eggs

2 tablespoons plain/all-purpose flour

FOR THE TOPPING

60 g/½ cup pine nuts

3 tablespoons honey

a 23-cm/9-inch round springform cake pan,
greased and lined

SERVES 12

Preheat the oven to 170°C (325°F) Gas 3.

To make the crumb base, crush the biscuits/graham crackers to fine crumbs in a food processor or place in a clean plastic bag and bash with a rolling pin. Transfer the crumbs to a mixing bowl and stir in the melted butter and pine nuts. Press the buttery crumbs into the base of the prepared cake pan firmly using the back of a spoon. Wrap the outside of the pan in cling film/plastic wrap and place in a roasting pan half full with water, ensuring that the water is not so high as to spill out. Set aside.

For the filling, whisk together the cream cheese, crème fraîche and the juice and zest of the lemons and lime in a large mixing bowl. Beat in the honey, sugar and eggs, then stir in the flour. Pour the mixture over the crumb base and transfer the cheesecake, in its waterbath, to the preheated oven. Bake for 1 – 1¼ hours until golden brown on top and still with a slight wobble in the centre. Remove the cheesecake from the waterbath and slide a knife around the edge of the pan to release the cheesecake and prevent it from cracking. Leave to cool, then transfer to the refrigerator to chill for at least 3 hours or preferably overnight.

For the topping, toast the pine nuts in a dry frying pan until lightly golden brown and sprinkle over the cheesecake. Heat the honey until just warm, then spoon over the cheesecake and serve.

crème brûlée cheesecakes

Tapping into a crispy sugar shell of a crème brûlée is one of life's little pleasures. These dainty cheesecakes are packed with vanilla and have a crunchy sugar topping that you can crack with a spoon. You need to be careful not to heat the sugar too much otherwise it will cause the cheesecakes to melt.

FOR THE CRUMB BASES

120 g/4 oz. caramelized biscuits/cookies (such as lotus)

60 g/4 tablespoons butter, melted

FOR THE FILLING

2 sheets leaf gelatine

250 g/generous 1 cup mascarpone cheese

60 g/scant ⅓ cup caster/white sugar

125 ml/½ cup double/heavy cream

1 teaspoon vanilla bean paste

caster/superfine sugar, to decorate

8 x 6-cm/2½-inch diameter chef's rings
a chef's blow torch

MAKES 8

For the bases, crush the biscuits/cookies to fine crumbs in a food processor or place in a clean plastic bag and bash with a rolling pin. Transfer the crumbs to a mixing bowl and stir in the melted butter. Place the chef's rings on a baking sheet and divide the crumbs evenly between the rings, pressing them down flat with the back of a spoon.

For the filling, soak the gelatine leaves in water until they are soft.

In a large mixing bowl, whisk together the mascarpone and sugar until light and creamy.

Heat the cream and vanilla in a heatproof bowl set over a pan of simmering water. Squeeze the water out of the gelatine leaves and add them to the warm cream, stirring until dissolved. Pass the cream through a sieve/strainer to remove any undissolved gelatine pieces, then whisk into the cheese mixture. Pour the filling mixture into the 8 rings and leave to set in the refrigerator for 3 hours or overnight.

When you are ready to serve, remove the cheesecakes from the rings by sliding a knife around the edge of each ring to release them. Place the cheesecakes in the freezer for 20 minutes to firm. Remove from the freezer and sprinkle the top of each cheesecake with a thin layer of sugar. Heat the sugar with the blow torch until it caramelizes, taking care not to overheat the cheesecakes otherwise they will start to melt. Let the cheesecakes come to room temperature before serving.

rose and cardamom cheesecake

FOR THE CAKE BASE

115 g/¾ cup shelled pistachios

60 g/scant ⅓ cup caster/white sugar

60 g/4 tablespoons butter, softened

2 eggs

60 g/scant ½ cup self-raising flour

FOR THE FILLING

6 sheets leaf gelatine

500 g/generous 2 cups ricotta

250 g/generous 1 cup mascarpone cheese

100 g/½ cup caster/white sugar

25 cardamom pods

300 g/1⅓ cups evaporated milk

160 ml/⅔ cup double/heavy cream

80 ml/⅓ cup rosewater

a few drops of pink food colouring
(optional)

FOR THE DECORATION

crystallized rose petals (see page 95)

2 tablespoons bright green pistachios,
chopped

edible glitter (optional)

a 23-cm/9-inch round springform cake pan,
greased and lined

SERVES 12

Rose and cardamom make one of my favourite flavour combinations. With a delicate pistachio sponge base and decorated with elegant rose petals and pistachios, this cheesecake makes a sophisticated dinner party dessert.

Preheat the oven to 180°C (350°F) Gas 4.

For the base, finely chop the pistachios in a food processor or blender.

In a large mixing bowl, whisk together the sugar and butter until creamy. Add the egg and beat again. Sift in the flour, add the ground pistachios and whisk well so that everything is incorporated. Pour the mixture into the prepared baking pan and bake in the preheated oven for 15–20 minutes until the cake is golden brown and springs back when pressed gently in the centre. Leave to cool in the pan.

For the cheesecake, soak the gelatine leaves in water until they are soft.

Whisk the ricotta, mascarpone cheese and sugar together until light and creamy. Crush the cardamom pods to remove the husks, then grind the black seeds to a fine powder in a pestle and mortar.

Heat the evaporated milk and cream together in a saucepan with the ground cardamom and rosewater and continue heating until the mixture has reduced by one third. Remove from the heat and leave to cool slightly. Squeeze the water out of the gelatine leaves and add them to the warm cream, stirring until dissolved. Pass the cream through a sieve/strainer to remove any undissolved gelatine pieces, then whisk into the cheese mixture with a few drops of pink food colouring, if using. Pour the filling on top of the pistachio cake base in the pan and leave to set in the refrigerator for 3 hours or overnight.

When you are ready to serve, arrange the crystallized rose petals on top of the cheesecake and sprinkle with chopped pistachios and edible glitter, if using.

crystallized flower cheesecakes

These cheesecakes are topped with pretty sugar flowers, which you can easily prepare yourself. Be careful to use only edible flowers that have not been sprayed with any chemicals or pesticides. Primroses, violets and rose petals all work well. They store well in an airtight container so can be made before you need them. To vary the cheesecakes to other floral themes you can omit the lavender and replace with either 3 tablespoons violet liqueur or 3 tablespoons rose syrup for equally delicious results.

FOR THE CRYSTALLIZED FLOWERS

1 egg white

pesticide-free edible flowers, stems removed

caster/superfine sugar for sprinkling

FOR THE CRUMB BASES

80 g/3 oz. digestive biscuits/graham crackers

40 g/3 tablespoons butter, melted

FOR THE FILLING

2 sheets leaf gelatine

250 g/generous 1 cup mascarpone cheese

60 g/scant ⅓ cup caster/white sugar

125 ml/½ cup double/heavy cream

2 teaspoons culinary lavender

a small paint brush

6 glass serving dishes

a silicone mat (optional)

MAKES 6

Begin by preparing the sugar flowers. Whisk the egg white until it is foamy. Working on one flower at a time, use the brush to paint the egg white on both the front and the back of the flower. Sprinkle it with caster/superfine sugar. (This is best done by holding the sugar at a small height above the flower and sprinkling lightly. Have a plate below to catch any excess sugar.) It is important that all the egg white is covered in sugar. Repeat with all the flowers and lay on a silicone mat or sheet of non-stick baking paper placed in a warm place to dry overnight. Once dried, stored the flowers in an airtight container until you are ready to serve.

To make the crumb bases, crush the biscuits/graham crackers to fine crumbs in a food processor or place in a clean plastic bag and bash with a rolling pin. Transfer the crumbs to a mixing bowl and stir in the melted butter. Press the buttery crumbs firmly into the base of each dish using the back of a spoon.

For the filling, soak the gelatine leaves in water until they are soft.

In a large mixing bowl, whisk the mascarpone and sugar together until light and creamy.

Put the cream in a heatproof bowl set over a pan of simmering water. Add the lavender and heat gently for about 5 minutes until the cream has taken the lavender flavour, then pass the cream through a sieve/strainer to remove the lavender buds. Reheat the cream until it is just warm. Squeeze the water out of the gelatine leaves and add them to the warm cream, stirring until the gelatine has dissolved. Pass the cream through a sieve/strainer a second time to remove any undissolved gelatine pieces, then whisk it into the cheese mixture. Pour the cheesecake mixture into the glasses and chill in the refrigerator for at least 3 hours.

When you are ready to serve, decorate each cheesecake with the crystallized flowers.

profiterole cheesecake

FOR THE BASE

250 g/9 oz. digestive biscuits/graham crackers

100 g/7 tablespoons butter, melted

FOR THE FILLING

300 g/1⅓ cups cream cheese

400 ml/1¾ cups crème fraîche

80 g/scant ½ cup caster/white sugar

2 eggs

1 teaspoon vanilla bean paste

FOR THE PROFITEROLES

65 g/½ cup plain/all-purpose flour

50 g/3½ tablespoons butter

2 eggs, beaten

FOR THE PATISSERIE CREAM

1 tablespoon cornflour/cornstarch

60 g/⅓ cup caster/white sugar

1 egg, plus 1 egg yolk

100 ml/generous ⅓ cup milk

150 ml/⅔ cup double/heavy cream

1 teaspoon vanilla extract

TO ASSEMBLE

200 ml/¾ cup double/heavy cream

80 g/scant ½ cup caster/white sugar

a 23-cm/9-inch round springform cake pan, greased and lined

a baking sheet, greased and lined

a piping bag fitted with a large round nozzle/tip

SERVES 14

Preheat the oven to 170°C (325°F) Gas 3.

For the base, crush the biscuits/graham crackers to fine crumbs in a food processor or place in a clean plastic bag and bash with a rolling pin. Transfer the crumbs to a mixing bowl and stir in the melted butter. Press the crumbs into the base of the cake pan firmly using the back of a spoon.

For the filling, whisk together the cream cheese, crème fraîche and sugar. Whisk in the eggs and vanilla, then pour over the crumb base. Bake in the preheated oven for 40–50 minutes until golden brown on top but still has a slight wobble in the centre. Leave to cool, then transfer to the refrigerator to chill for at least 3 hours or preferably overnight.

For the profiteroles, preheat the oven to 200°C (400°F) Gas 6. Sift the flour twice to remove any lumps. Heat the butter and 150 ml/⅔ cup water in a saucepan until the butter is melted. Bring to the boil, then add the flour, remove from the heat and beat hard with a wooden spoon until the dough forms a ball and no longer sticks to the pan sides. Leave to cool for about 5 minutes. Whisk the eggs into the pastry, a little at a time, to form a sticky paste. Spoon into the piping bag and pipe 45 small balls onto the baking sheet. Wet your finger and smooth down any peaks then bake in the oven for 12 minutes. Remove from the oven and cut a small slit into each bun and return to the oven for 3–5 minutes until crisp. Leave to cool on a rack.

For the pâtisserie cream, whisk together the cornflour/cornstarch, sugar, egg and egg yolk until creamy. Put the milk, cream and the vanilla in a saucepan and bring to the boil. Pour over the egg mixture, whisking all the time. Return to the pan and cook for a few minutes until thickened. Pass through a sieve/strainer to remove any lumps, then leave to cool.

To assemble the cheesecake, whisk the 200 ml/⅔ cup cream to stiff peaks, then fold through the pâtisserie cream. Spread some of the pâtisserie cream over the top of the cheesecake and spoon the rest into the piping bag. Fill each profiterole with the cream, piping it into the slit in the profiterole, then arrange them in rings on top of the cheesecake.

For the spun sugar, heat the sugar in a heavy-based saucepan until it caramelizes (watching carefully as it easily burns). Do not stir the sugar but gently shake the pan to prevent it from burning. Allow the caramel to cool slightly until the sugar becomes tacky and threads pull when you lift up a spoon from it. Pull threads of caramel by starting with some of the slightly cooled caramel on a spoon and allowing a drip to fall to create a sugar thread, then keep pulling the thread with your fingers (taking care as the caramel in the spoon will be hot) to create the spun sugar. If the caramel becomes too solid, simply return to the heat for a few seconds and then continue as before. Wrap the spun sugar into a ball and place on top of the profiteroles. Serve immediately

crunchy almond cheesecake

There was a chef where I worked in London many years ago who made the best amaretto baked peaches I have ever eaten, with a marzipan amaretti biscuit topping. The heady combination is one of my favourite things to eat and I don't even like marzipan! I have used that topping to give this almond cheesecake a crunchy crust – a perfect contrast to the creamy almond filling. If you wish you can serve some poached peaches to accompany this cheesecake, or freshly whipped cream flavoured with amaretto.

FOR THE NUTTY CRUST

150 g/scant 2 cups flaked/slivered almonds

30 g/2 tablespoons butter, softened

FOR THE FILLING

500 g/generous 2 cups cream cheese

500 g/generous 2 cups ricotta

4 large eggs

400 g/1¾ cups condensed milk

80 g/⅓ cup almond butter

1 teaspoon almond extract

FOR THE TOPPING

80 g/¾ stick butter

120 g/½ cup golden marzipan (or white marzipan if golden is not available)

100 g/scant 1 cup crushed amaretti biscuits/cookies

a 23-cm/9-inch round springform cake pan, greased and lined

SERVES 12

In a dry frying pan set over a gentle heat, toast the flaked/slivered almonds until lightly golden brown, watching carefully as almonds can burn quickly. Tip into a bowl and set aside to cool completely.

Spread the softened butter around the sides and base of the prepared cake pan. Sprinkle the cooled toasted almonds into the pan and shake it so that the base and sides of the pan are covered with almonds. (Do not try to do this whilst the almonds are hot or they will melt the butter and not stick to the sides of the pan.)

Preheat the oven to 170°C (325°F) Gas 3.

In a large mixing bowl, whisk together the cream cheese and ricotta, then add the eggs, condensed milk, almond butter and almond extract and whisk until the mixture is smooth. Spoon the mixture into the almond-coated pan and bake in the preheated oven for 45 minutes.

Whilst the cheesecake is baking, prepare the topping. Melt the butter in a saucepan. Chop the marzipan into small pieces and mix with the crushed amaretti biscuits/cookies. Pour over the warm melted butter and mix together. For best results do this with your hands so that the biscuits/cookies and marzipan stick together in small clumps.

After 45 minutes baking time, the cheesecake should be golden brown on top and still wobble slightly in the centre. Carefully sprinkle the marzipan crumbs over the top of the cheesecake (this is best done with the cheesecake still in the oven but only if you can do so safely without burning yourself). Bake for a further 15 minutes until the topping is crunchy and the marzipan has caramelized. Remove the cheesecake from the oven and slide a knife gently around the edge of the pan to loosen the cheesecake and prevent it from cracking. Leave to cool, then chill in the refrigerator for at least 3 hours or overnight before serving.

cheesecake chocolates

Dainty cheesecake chocolates, served in a classic chocolate box, are the perfect petit fours to serve at the end of a meal. These are flavoured with hints of vanilla and orange but you can vary to any flavour you prefer. The creamy cheesecake filling comes as an unexpected surprise when you bite into the crisp chocolate shell. You may not need to use all of the cake batter, but you can bake the remainder into a few cupcakes, if you wish.

FOR THE CAKE BASES

55 g/4 tablespoons butter

55 g/4½ tablespoons caster/white sugar

1 egg

55 g/scant ½ cup self-raising flour

grated zest of 1 orange

FOR THE DRIZZLING SYRUP

freshly squeezed juice of 1 orange

1 tablespoon icing/confectioners' sugar

FOR THE FILLING

170 g/¾ cup mascarpone cheese

170 ml/¾ cup crème fraîche

1 tablespoon icing/confectioners' sugar

1 teaspoon vanilla bean paste

TO ASSEMBLE

400 g/14 oz. dark spiced chocolate (such as Green & Black's Maya Gold)

24 sugar flowers

a 24-hole square mini brownie pan, greased

a piping bag fitted with a round nozzle/tip (optional)

24 paper petit fours cases

MAKES 24

Preheat the oven to 180°C (350°F) Gas 4.

To make the cake bases, whisk together the butter and sugar in a large mixing bowl, until light and creamy. Beat in the egg and whisk again. Sift in the flour, add half of the orange zest and stir through again. Put a small spoonful of mixture into each of the holes of the prepared brownie pan. (This is easiest done with a piping bag.) You only want a little cake mixture in each hole as when the cakes are baked you still need room to add the cheesecake mixture on top. Bake in the preheated oven for 10–12 minutes until the sponges spring back when you press with a clean finger.

Simmer the orange juice and sugar in a saucepan until the sugar has dissolved, then drizzle a little of the syrup over each of the cakes. Leave the cakes to cool, then press the cakes down so that there is room for the filling on top.

For the cheesecake filling, whisk together the mascarpone, crème fraîche, icing/confectioners' sugar, vanilla and the remaining orange zest until smooth. Spoon the mixture over the cake bases, spreading in tightly using a pallet knife or spatula so that all the holes of the brownie pan are filled completely. Transfer the pan to the freezer and freeze until the cheesecake is solid, which will take about 30 minutes.

When the cheesecakes are frozen, melt the dark chocolate in a heatproof bowl set over a pan of simmering water, stirring until the chocolate has melted. Remove the frozen cheesecakes from the freezer and, one at a time, dip them into the warm chocolate. Transfer to a wire rack to set, with a sheet of foil underneath to catch any chocolate drips. Before the chocolate sets, affix a sugar flower to the top of each cheesecake. The chocolate will set quickly given the frozen temperatures of the cheesecakes – if it sets too quickly you can simply attach the flowers using a little extra chocolate. Once set, place each chocolate in a petit fours case and store in the refrigerator until you are ready to serve, by which time the cheesecake will have defrosted.

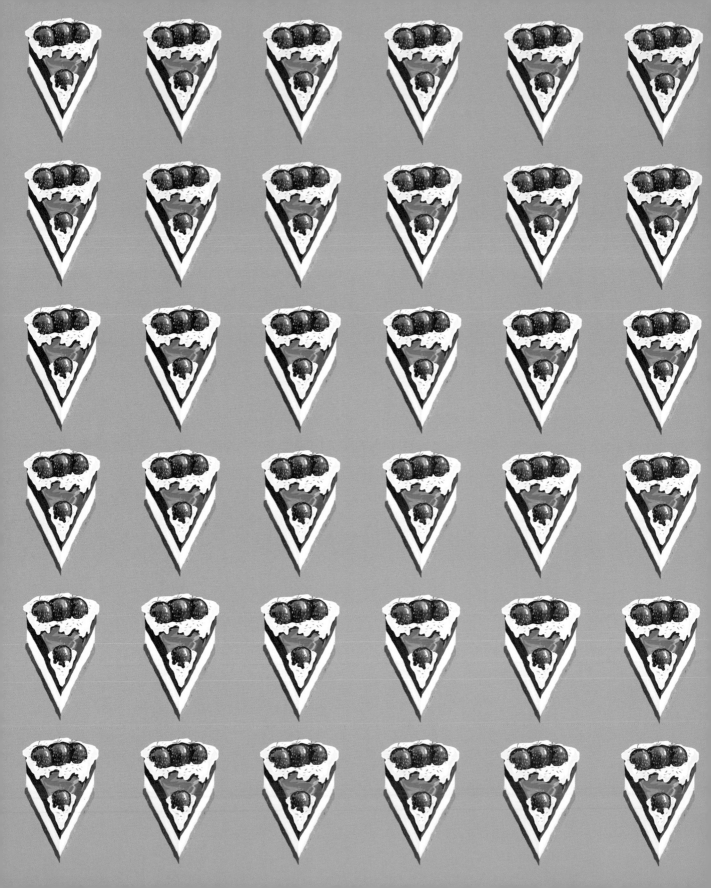

party cheesecakes

trifle cheesecakes

These little cheesecakes, served in cute jars, are my cheesecake twist on the classic English trifle dessert. Delicate slices of jam Swiss roll/jelly roll are drizzled with amaretto, sprinkled with raspberries and topped with cheesecake in place of the traditional whipped cream and custard. These little jars transport well for picnics and make a special treat in packed lunches.

1 small raspberry jam Swiss roll/jelly roll

200 g/1½ cups fresh raspberries

3 generous tablespoons amaretto or almond liqueur

65 g/2½ oz. raspberry jelly cubes/jello powder

250 g/generous 1 cup mascarpone cheese

250 ml/1 cup sour cream

2 tablespoons icing/confectioners' sugar, or to taste

1 teaspoon vanilla bean paste

sugar sprinkles, to decorate

6 small kilner jars or jam jars with lids

a piping bag fitted with a large round nozzle/tip

SERVES 6

Cut the swiss roll/jelly roll into thin slices, then cut each slice in half. Arrange the slices around the sides of each jar and a slice in the base. Sprinkle over the raspberries and drizzle with the amaretto.

Make up the raspberry jelly/jello according to the package instructions and pour it into the jars, dividing it equally between them. Leave to set in the refrigerator.

Once the jelly/jello has set, prepare the cheesecake topping. In a large mixing bowl, whisk together the mascarpone and sour cream until smooth. Sift the icing/confectioners' sugar over the mixture, add the vanilla paste, and fold through, testing for sweetness and adding a little more icing/confectioners' sugar if you prefer.

Spoon the cheese mixture into the piping bag and pipe blobs on top of each trifle, making sure that the jelly/jello is covered completely. Decorate with sugar sprinkles to serve.

baked Alaska cheesecakes

FOR THE CRUMB BASES

120 g/4 oz. chocolate digestives/graham crackers

50 g/3½ tablespoons butter

FOR THE FILLING

2 sheets leaf gelatine

250 g/generous 1 cup mascarpone cheese

50 g/¼ cup caster/white sugar

80 ml/⅓ cup passion fruit pulp, strained (about 8 passion fruit)

125 ml/½ cup double/heavy cream

a few drops of orange food colouring (optional)

FOR THE SORBET

150 g/¾ cup granulated sugar

150 g/5½ oz. dark chocolate

60 g/⅔ cup cocoa powder, sifted

1 teaspoon vanilla extract

½ teaspoon salt

FOR THE MERINGUE

200 g/1 cup caster/superfine sugar

80 ml/⅓ cup light corn syrup (if unavailable, use golden syrup)

4 egg whites

8 x 6-cm/2½-inch chef's rings

an ice cream machine (optional)

a sugar thermometer

a chef's blow torch (optional)

MAKES 8

These individual baked Alaskas have a perfect combination of creamy passion fruit cheesecake topped with ice cold chocolate sorbet all wrapped up in toasted hot meringue. There is more sorbet than needed for the baked Alaska recipe, but it makes a useful standby dessert.

For the crumb bases, crush the biscuits/graham crackers to fine crumbs in a food processor or place in a clean plastic bag and bash with a rolling pin. Transfer the crumbs to a mixing bowl and stir in the melted butter. Place the chef's rings on a baking sheet and divide the buttery crumbs between them, pressing them down firmly with the back of a spoon.

To make the filling, soak the gelatine leaves in water until they are soft.

In a large mixing bowl, whisk together the mascarpone and sugar until light and creamy, then whisk in the passion fruit juice.

Put the cream in a heatproof bowl set over a pan of simmering water and warm gently. Squeeze the water out of the gelatine leaves and add them to the warm cream, stirring until dissolved. Pass the cream through a sieve/strainer to remove any undissolved gelatine pieces, then whisk into the cheese mixture with a few drops of orange food colouring, if using. Pour the cheesecake mixture into the 8 chef's rings and leave to set in the refrigerator for 3 hours or overnight.

To prepare the sorbet, simmer the sugar with 500 ml/2 cups water in a saucepan until you have a thin syrup. Add the chocolate, cocoa, vanilla and salt to the pan and simmer until the chocolate has melted. Leave to cool completely, then churn in an ice cream machine until frozen. If you do not have an ice cream machine, transfer to a box, place in the freezer and whisk every 20 minutes to break up the ice crystals until frozen. Scoop 8 round balls of sorbet and store on a tray in the freezer until you are ready to serve. (Store any leftover sorbet in the freezer for another day.)

For the meringue, simmer the sugar and syrup together with 110 ml/⅓ cup water until the sugar has dissolved, then bring to the boil and, using a sugar thermometer, heat the syrup to 115°C (242°F) or soft ball stage.

In a clean dry bowl, whisk the egg whites to stiff peaks, then add the hot sugar syrup in a small drizzle whisking continuously. Whisk for about 10–15 minutes until the meringue starts to cool.

When you are ready to serve, remove the cheesecakes from the rings by sliding a sharp knife around the edge of each. Place each on a heatproof serving plate and top with a scoop of sorbet. Working quickly, spread the meringue around each cheesecake using a pallet knife, then caramelize it with the chef's blow torch or brown under a grill/broiler. Serve immediately!

mini popcorn cheesecakes

As you may have gathered from my last book, *Popcorn Treats*, I am a sucker for popcorn. It is such a fun snack and really is irresistible. These mini cheesecakes have tiny pieces of popcorn in the base and are topped with a mound of popcorn and toffee sauce. If you use homemade popcorn, make sure that all the unpopped kernels are removed before using as they are an unwelcome addition if you bite into one.

FOR THE CRUMB BASES

80 g/3 oz. digestive biscuits/graham crackers

50 g/2 oz. toffee-coated popcorn (such as Butterkist)

70 g/5 tablespoons butter, melted

FOR THE FILLING

250 g/generous 1 cup cream cheese

250 g/generous 1 cup mascarpone cheese

2 small eggs

1 teaspoon vanilla bean paste or vanilla extract

200 g/scant 1 cup condensed milk

FOR THE TOPPING

25 g/2 tablespoons caster/white sugar

25 g/2 tablespoons muscovado sugar

25 g/1¾ tablespoons butter

80 ml/⅓ cup double/heavy cream

50 g/2 oz. toffee-coated popcorn

a 12-hole loose-based mini cheesecake pan or muffin pan (with 5-cm/2-inch holes), greased

12 muffin wrappers (optional)

MAKES 12

Preheat the oven to 170°C (325°F) Gas 3.

For the bases, crush the biscuits/graham crackers and popcorn to fine crumbs in a food processor or place in a clean plastic bag and bash with a rolling pin. Transfer the crumbs to a mixing bowl and stir in the melted butter. Place a spoonful of the crumbs in each hole of the cheesecake pan and press down firmly using the end of a rolling pin or the back of a small spoon. Retain a little of the crumb mixture to sprinkle over the cheesecakes.

For the filling, whisk together the cream cheese and mascarpone in a large mixing bowl. Add the eggs, vanilla and condensed milk and whisk again until smooth. Pour the mixture into the 12 holes of the pan so that they are almost full. (Depending on the size of your pan you may not need all of the mixture.) Sprinkle the reserved crumbs over the top of each cheesecake and bake in the preheated oven for 20–25 minutes until set with a slight wobble. Once cool, remove from the pan and chill in the refrigerator for several hours.

For the topping, heat the sugars and butter in a saucepan until the sugars have dissolved. Add the cream and heat gently until you have a thick caramel sauce. Set aside to cool.

When you are ready to serve, place the cheesecakes in the muffin wrappers, if using, or on a serving plate. Spoon a little of the caramel sauce over each cheesecake and top with popcorn. Serve any remaining sauce alongside for extra drizzling.

berry sundae cheesecakes

These little layered cheesecakes are perfect as a pre-dessert or as part of a dessert trio. I have used strawberries but you can use a variety of other fruits – kiwi, raspberries, nectarines and blueberries all work well – and if you prefer, substitute digestive biscuits/graham crackers for the Oreo crumbs. The possibilities for variations of this little cheesecake are endless!

FOR THE FRUITY LAYER

2 tablespoons vanilla vodka (optional)

12 strawberries, quartered

FOR THE CRUMBLY LAYER

8 Oreo cookies

1 generous tablespoon butter, melted

FOR THE CHEESECAKE LAYER

125 g/½ cup mascarpone cheese

125 ml/½ cup crème fraîche

1 teaspoon vanilla bean paste

1 generous tablespoon icing/confectioners' sugar

TO ASSEMBLE

150 ml/⅔ cup double/heavy cream, whipped

chocolate sprinkles

6 small glasses

a piping bag fitted with a round nozzle/tip (optional)

a piping bag fitted with a star nozzle/tip

MAKES 6

If using the vodka, place the chopped strawberries in a bowl, pour over the vodka and leave to macerate, covered with cling film/plastic wrap, for about 20 minutes.

To make the crumbly layer, crush the Oreo cookies to fine crumbs in a food processor or place in a clean plastic bag and bash with a rolling pin. Transfer the crumbs to a mixing bowl and stir in the melted butter, ensuring that all the crumbs are coated.

In a large mixing bowl, whisk together the mascarpone cheese and crème fraîche, then beat in the vanilla bean paste and icing/confectioners' sugar. Spoon the cheese mixture into the piping bag fitted with the round nozzle/tip, if using.

Place a teaspoon of the cookie crumb mixture in the base of each glass. Pipe in a small amount of the cream cheese mixture and top with a teaspoon of strawberry pieces. (You can add the cheese mixture with a spoon if you wish.) Continue to layer up the cheesecakes until you have filled the glasses, then chill in the refrigerator until you are ready to serve.

To serve, spoon the whipped cream into the piping bag fitted with the star nozzle/tip and pipe a swirl of cream on top of each sundae, then decorate with chocolate sprinkles. Once chilled, they are best eaten the day they are made.

valentine heart cheesecakes

These delicious fruity cheesecakes, enclosed in delicate swirled heart meringues are wonderful for a romantic supper. Filled with cherries and creamy mascarpone, they are a perfect light dessert. One is definitely not enough.

FOR THE MERINGUE HEARTS

3 egg whites

170 g/scant 1 cup caster/superfine sugar

a few drops of pink food colouring gel

FOR THE FILLING

250 g/generous 1 cup mascarpone cheese

200 ml/generous ¾ cup crème fraîche

100 g/⅓ cup cherry compôte

2 tablespoons icing/confectioners' sugar, sifted

TO ASSEMBLE

6 tablespoons cherry compôte

crystallized rose petals (see page 95), shredded

a 6-hole silicone heart mould (each heart approx 6 cm/2½ inches in size)

a large baking sheet lined with baking parchment or a silicone mat

a piping bag fitted with a large round nozzle/tip

MAKES 6

Preheat the oven to 140°C (275°F) Gas 1.

Put the egg whites in a large mixing bowl and whisk until they hold stiff peaks. Add the sugar, a tablespoonful at a time, whisking constantly, until the meringue is shiny and glossy. Fold through the food colouring, stopping before it is fully incorporated to leave pretty swirls in the meringue.

Spoon the meringue into the piping bag and pipe 12 heart shapes, about 7 cm/3 inches in length onto the baking sheets. (You want the hearts to be just slightly larger than the size of your cheesecake moulds.) Bake the hearts in the preheated oven for about 1 – 1¼ hours until the meringue is dried and crisp, then leave to cool.

For the cheesecake filling, whisk together the mascarpone and crème fraîche in a large mixing bowl. Fold the cherry compôte into the cheese mixture along with the icing/confectioners' sugar. Spoon the mixture into each heart in the mould and place in the freezer.

When frozen, pop the hearts out of the mould and leave to defrost slightly. Place a spoonful of cherry compôte onto 6 of the meringues and top each with a cheesecake heart. Place a second meringue heart on top of the cheesecake and decorate with shredded rose petals to serve.

jelly and custard cheesecake

Jelly/jello and custard – a favourite children's party dessert – is the inspiration for this wibbly wobbly cheesecake. My version is made with strawberry jelly and fresh strawberries but you could vary the ingredients and use raspberry jelly and fresh raspberries or lime jelly and candied lime slices if you prefer.

FOR THE TOPPING

135 g-packet strawberry jelly cubes/3-oz. box strawberry jello powder

1 teaspoon vanilla bean paste

150 ml/⅔ cup double/heavy cream, whipped to stiff peaks

8 strawberries, hulled and sliced, plus 1 whole strawberry

sugar sprinkles, to decorate

FOR THE CRUMB BASE

200 g/7 oz. pink wafer biscuits

60 g/4 tablespoons butter, melted

FOR THE CHEESECAKE

4 sheets leaf gelatine

300 g/1⅓ cups cream cheese

250 g/generous 1 cup mascarpone cheese

100 g/½ cup vanilla sugar

180 ml/¾ cup double/heavy cream

1 generous tablespoon custard powder/ vanilla pudding mix

an 18-cm/7-inch ring silicone jelly mould

a 23-cm/9-inch round springform cake pan, greased and lined

a piping bag fitted with a star nozzle/tip

SERVES 10

Begin by preparing the jelly/jello topping. You need to do this the day before you want to serve the cheesecake as it is best to set overnight. Make up the jelly/jello according to the package instructions and stir the vanilla into the liquid. Pour the jelly/jello into the mould and leave to set.

For the base, crush the wafers to fine crumbs in a food processor or place in a clean plastic bag and bash with a rolling pin. Transfer the crumbs to a mixing bowl and stir in the melted butter. Press the buttery crumbs into the base of the prepared cake pan firmly using the back of a spoon until tightly compacted.

For the filling, soak the gelatine leaves in water until they are soft.

In a large mixing bowl, whisk together the cream cheese, mascarpone and sugar until light and creamy.

Put the cream in a heatproof bowl set over a pan of simmering water and warm gently. Stir in the custard powder/vanilla pudding mix and whisk until blended. Squeeze the water from the gelatine leaves and stir them into the cream until the gelatine dissolves. Carefully add the cream to the cream cheese mixture passing it through a sieve/strainer to remove any gelatine pieces that have not dissolved, then beat until the mixture is smooth and slightly thick. Pour the mixture over the crumb base and chill in the refrigerator for 3–4 hours or overnight until set.

When you are ready to serve, remove the cheesecake from the pan by sliding a knife around the edge of the pan and transfer the cheesecake to a serving plate. Dip the jelly/jello mould in a bowl of hot water for a few seconds to loosen the jelly/jello from the sides of the mould. Invert the jelly/jello mould on to the top of the cheesecake and remove the mould.

Spoon the whipped cream into the piping bag and pipe stars around the edge of the cheesecake, then pipe a little into the centre of the jelly/jello. Arrange slices of strawberry around the edge of the jelly/jello and place the whole strawberry in the centre. Decorate with sugar sprinkles and serve straight away.

macaron cheesecakes

FOR THE MACARONS

120 g/1¼ cups ground almonds

175 g/1¼ cups icing/confectioners' sugar

90 g/3 oz. egg whites (about 3 eggs)

75 g/generous ⅓ cup caster/superfine sugar

orange food colouring gel

FOR THE CRUMB BASES

150 g/5½ oz. digestive biscuits/graham crackers

70 g/⅔ stick butter

FOR THE FILLING

2 sheets leaf gelatine

250 g/generous 1 cup mascarpone cheese

50 g/¼ cup caster/white sugar

freshly squeezed juice and grated zest of 1 large orange

freshly squeezed juice of 1 lemon

125 ml/½ cup double/heavy cream

a few drops of orange food colouring

TO ASSEMBLE

1 tablespoon lemon curd

200 ml/¾ cup double/heavy cream, whipped to stiff peaks

edible gold dusting powder

a piping bag fitted with a round nozzle/tip

2 baking sheets lined with silicone mats

a 12-hole loose-based mini cheesecake pan (with 5-cm/2-inch holes), greased

a piping bag fitted with a star nozzle/tip

MAKES 12

The pretty macarons on these cheesecakes are flavoured with citrus but you can vary the flavour and colour to whatever takes your fancy, or go for a variety of colours for a pretty effect.

For the macarons, put the ground almonds and icing/confectioners' sugar in a food processor and blitz to a very fine powder. Sift into a bowl and return any pieces that do not pass through the sieve/strainer to the blender, blitz, then sift again.

Whisk the egg whites to stiff peaks, then add the caster/superfine sugar a spoonful at a time until the meringue is smooth and glossy. Add the almond mixture, a third at a time, folding in with a spatula, then fold in the food colouring. The right texture is important – drop a little onto a plate and if it folds to a smooth surface it is ready; if it holds a peak you need to fold it a few further times. If you fold it too much it will be too runny and the macarons will not hold their shape. Spoon the mixture into the piping bag with the round nozzle/tip and pipe 24 5-cm/2-inch rounds onto the baking sheets, with a little space around each. Leave on the sheets for 20 minutes so that a skin forms on the macarons, which will give them their classic sugar-crusted edge. Preheat the oven to 170°C (325°F) Gas 3 and bake them for 15–20 minutes until firm. Leave to cool on the baking sheets.

To make the crumb bases, crush the biscuits/graham crackers to fine crumbs in a food processor or place in a clean plastic bag and bash with a rolling pin. Transfer the crumbs to a mixing bowl and stir in the melted butter. Divide the buttery crumbs between the holes of the cheesecake pan and press firmly down with the end of a rolling pin or the back of a spoon.

For the filling, soak the gelatine leaves in water until they are soft.

In a large mixing bowl, whisk the mascarpone and sugar together until light and creamy. Whisk in the orange and lemon juice and orange zest.

Heat the cream in a heatproof bowl set over a pan of simmering water. Squeeze the water out of the gelatine leaves and add them to the warm cream, stirring until dissolved. Pass through a sieve/strainer to remove any undissolved gelatine pieces, then whisk into the cheese mixture with a few drops of orange food colouring, if using. Pour the cheesecake mixture into the holes of the pan and leave to set in the refrigerator for at least 3 hours.

To assemble, carefully remove the cheesecakes from the pan. Fold the lemon curd through the whipped cream and spoon into the piping bag. Pipe a star of cream onto the base of 12 of the macarons and sandwich them with the other 12. Pipe a small dot of cream into the centre of each cheesecake and place a filled macaron onto each. Brush the tops of the macarons with the gold dusting powder using a dry pastry brush. Serve immediately or store in the refrigerator until needed.

toasted marshmallow cheesecake pie

I have fond memories of toasting marshmallows on beach holidays when we were young. When toasted, these sweets become absolutely delicious, with their caramel coating and a gooey soft centre. This cheesecake pie is inspired by those holiday memories, topped with a caramelized marshmallow topping with marshmallows in the crumb crust, too. Very naughty, but so very nice!

FOR THE CRUMB CASE

140 g/5 oz. Oreo cookies

140 g/5 oz. chocolate digestive biscuits/graham crackers

6 chocolate marshmallow teacakes (such as Tunnock's or Dickmann's)

100 g/7 tablespoons butter, melted

FOR THE FILLING

6 sheets leaf gelatine

300 g/1⅓ cups cream cheese

250 g/geneous 1 cup mascarpone cheese

50 g/¼ cup caster/white sugar

1 teaspoon vanilla bean paste or vanilla extract

300 ml/1¼ cups double/heavy cream

200 g/7 oz. dark chocolate, broken into small pieces

250 g/6-7 cups marshmallows

a 23-cm/9-inch round springform cake pan, greased and lined

SERVES 12

For the crumb case, crush all the biscuits/cookies and teacakes to fine crumbs in a food processor. Transfer the crumbs to a mixing bowl and stir in the melted butter. Press the buttery crumbs into the base and sides of the prepared cake pan firmly using the back of a spoon. You need the crumbs to come up about 3-4 cm/1½ inches high on the side of the pan so that they make a case for the filling. Make indents in the top edge of the case with your fingers to create a pretty scalloped edge.

For the filling, soak the gelatine leaves in water until they are soft.

In a large mixing bowl, whisk together the cream cheese, mascarpone, sugar and vanilla until light and creamy.

Put the cream in a heatproof bowl set over a saucepan of simmering water and heat gently. Squeeze the water from the gelatine leaves and stir them into the warm cream until the gelatine has dissolved. Add the broken chocolate pieces to the cream and simmer until the chocolate has melted. Pass the chocolatey cream through a sieve/strainer to remove any undissolved gelatine pieces, then whisk into the cheese mixture until smooth. Spoon the mixture into the crumb case and chill in the refrigerator for about 3 hours or overnight until set.

When you are ready to serve, preheat the grill/broiler. Cut the marshmallows in half and arrange them over the top of the cheesecake so that they are touching. Place the cheesecake under the preheated grill/broiler for a few minutes until the marshmallows just start to caramelize. (If you cook them for too long they will melt and pour down the sides of the cheesecake when you remove the ring, which will still taste nice but won't look quite as pretty.) Slide a knife around the edge of the cheesecake and remove from the pan. Serve immediately.

cheesecake pops

These mini cheesecake bites served as lollipops are great for a children's party as you can decorate them with cheerful multicoloured sprinkles. They can be prepared in advance and kept in the refrigerator until just before serving. I have flavoured these with cinnamon but you could replace the cinnamon with finely grated lemon or orange zest if you prefer.

FOR THE CHEESECAKE

300 g/1⅓ cups cream cheese

150 ml/⅔ cup sour cream

100 g/½ cup caster/white sugar

2 eggs

1 teaspoon vanilla bean paste
or vanilla extract

2 teaspoons ground cinnamon

50 g/generous ⅓ cup self-raising flour

FOR THE DECORATION

200 g/7 oz. white chocolate

200 g/7 oz. dark chocolate

sugar sprinkles

a 20-cm/8-inch square loose-based cake
pan, greased and lined

3 or 4-cm/1½-inch round cookie cutter

white lollipop/popsicle sticks

a silicone mat (optional)

MAKES ABOUT 20

Preheat the oven to 170°C (325°F) Gas 3.

To prepare the cheesecake, whisk together the cream cheese, sour cream, sugar, eggs, vanilla, cinnamon and flour in a large mixing bowl until you have a smooth creamy mixture. Pour the mixture into the prepared cake pan and bake in the preheated oven for 35–45 minutes until the top is golden brown but still wobbles slightly in the centre. Remove from the oven and leave to cool.

When cold, remove the cheesecake from the pan and stamp out rounds using the cutter (you should be able to make about 20). Insert a lollipop/popsicle stick into each cheesecake round and place them on a baking sheet. Freeze for 30 minutes or until solid.

Melt the white chocolate in a heatproof bowl set over a pan of simmering water. Remove half the cheesecakes from the freezer and dip into the warm chocolate. Cover with sugar sprinkles and leave to set on a silicone mat, if using, or sheet of non-stick baking paper. (It is best to decorate the pops one at a time as the chocolate will set quickly on the cold cheesecake.) Repeat with the dark chocolate, dipping and decorating the remaining cheesecakes.

Store in the refrigerator until you are ready to serve.

pear and praline push pop cheesecakes

Push pops are a new and quirky concept which are sure to bring a smile! There are quite a few steps to this recipe but they can be prepared ahead and just assembled at the last minute.

FOR THE CHOCOLATE SHORTCAKES

100 g/¾ cup plain/all-purpose flour

30 g/⅓ cup cocoa powder

30 g/2½ tablespoons caster/white sugar

½ teaspoon salt

75 g/5 tablespoons butter, softened

FOR THE PEARS

3 ripe pears, peeled, cored and chopped into small pieces

freshly squeezed juice of 1 lemon

50 g/¼ cup sugar

FOR THE PRALINE AND CANDIED NUTS

150 g/1 cup macadamia nuts

150 g/¾ cup caster/white sugar

FOR THE FILLING

250 g/generous 1 cup mascarpone cheese

250 ml/1 cup crème fraîche

1 teaspoon vanilla bean paste

2 tablespoons icing/confectioners' sugar, sifted

a cookie cutter slightly smaller than the diameter of the push pops

12 wooden skewers

a silicone mat (optional)

a piping bag fitted with a star nozzle/tip

12 push pops

MAKES 12

For the shortcakes, sift the flour and cocoa powder in a large mixing bowl and stir in the sugar and salt. Rub the butter into the mixture with your finger tips until you have a soft dough, adding a little more flour if the mixture is too sticky. Wrap the dough in cling film/plastic wrap and chill in the refrigerator for 30 minutes. Meanwhile, preheat the oven to 180°C (350°F) Gas 4.

Roll out the dough thinly on a sheet of non-stick baking paper and transfer the paper to a baking sheet. Bake for 10–12 minutes until firm but still slightly soft. Let the shortcake cool for a few minutes, then stamp out 24 rounds with the cutter. (You can cut the cookies before baking but they will spread during cooking so may then not fit your pops.) Leave the cookies to cool.

Simmer the pear pieces in a saucepan with the lemon juice, sugar and 60 ml/¼ cup water until the pears are soft but still hold their shape (about 5–8 minutes). Strain off the liquid and leave the pears to cool.

For the praline, insert 12 of the macadamia nuts onto the skewers and set aside. Place the remaining nuts closely together on a silicone mat or greased baking sheet. Heat the sugar in a heavy-based saucepan until it caramelizes (watch carefully as it burns easily). Do not stir the sugar but gently shake the pan to prevent it from burning. Pour two thirds of the sugar over the nuts and leave to set. Allow the remaining sugar to cool slightly until it becomes tacky and threads pull when you lift up a spoon from it. One at a time, dip the skewered nuts into the sugar, coating completely and then pull upwards so that a thread of caramel pulls from the top of the nut. Let the caramel set for a few minutes with the nut held downwards (it's useful to have someone to help you hold them while you carry on dipping the remaining nuts). If the caramel in the pan becomes too solid, simply return to the heat for a few seconds, then continue as before. Once cool, remove the whole macadamias from the sticks and store in an airtight container until you are ready to assemble. Blitz the sheet of praline nuts in a food processor to make fine praline crumbs.

For the cheesecake filling, whisk together the mascarpone, crème fraiche, vanilla and icing/confectioners' sugar until the mixture thickens and holds a soft peak when you lift up the beater. Spoon the mixture into the piping bag.

When you are ready to serve, assemble the push pops. Make sure that the push up part is correctly inserted into the base of each pop container. Spoon a few pieces of pear into the base of each push pop, sprinkle with praline dust, pipe in some of the cheesecake filling, then cover with a shortcake. Repeat the layers, ending with a cream star on top of each pop. Place one of the caramelized macadamias on top of each pop – insert the push stick and serve immediately.

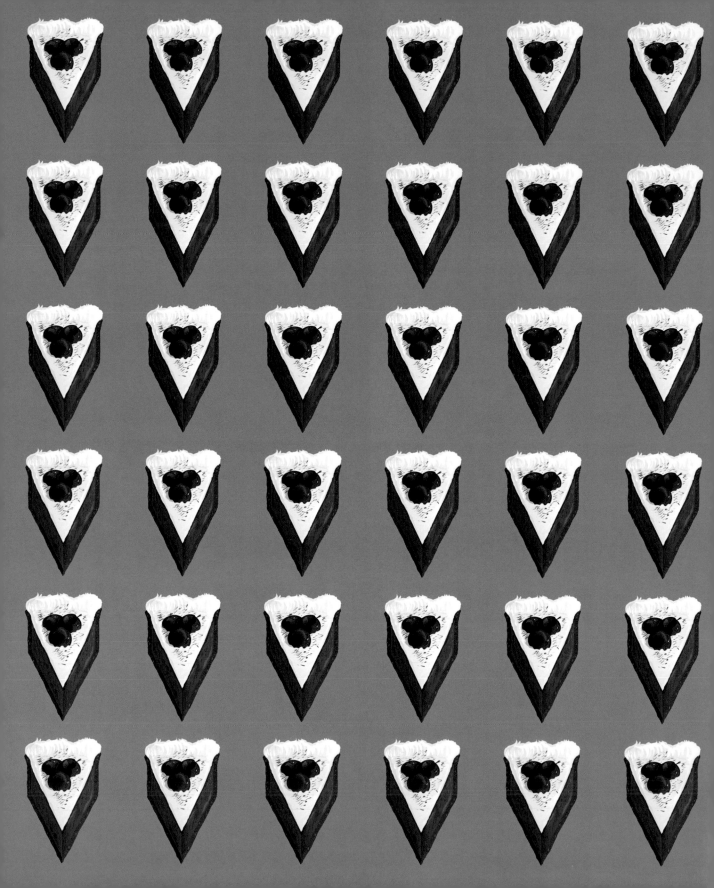

around the world
cheesecakes

· ·

American pumpkin cheesecake

Pumpkin is one of the staple ingredients of a Thanksgiving dessert in America. Whilst usually baked into a classic pumpkin pie, this cheesecake – packed with pumpkin purée and lots of fragrant spices – would make a perfect alternative. You can serve the cheesecake with fresh berries and extra cream if you wish. I use Libby's pumpkin purée but you can prepare your own purée by following my tip below.

FOR THE BASE

200 g/7 oz. digestive biscuits/graham crackers

100 g/7 tablespoons butter, melted

FOR THE FILLING

600 g/2⅔ cups cream cheese

225 g/1 cup clotted cream (use crème fraîche if not available)

160 ml/⅔ cup double/heavy cream

100 g/½ cup caster/white sugar

425 g/1¾ cups pumpkin purée

4 eggs

2 teaspoons ground cinnamon

1 teaspoon mixed/apple pie spice

1 teaspoon vanilla bean paste

TO SERVE

icing/confectioners' sugar and ground cinnamon, for dusting

whipped cream

a 26-cm/10-inch round springform cake pan, greased and lined

SERVES 12

Preheat the oven to 170°C (325°F) Gas 3.

To make the crumb base, crush the biscuits/graham crackers to fine crumbs in a food processor or place in a clean plastic bag and bash with a rolling pin. Transfer the crumbs to a mixing bowl and stir in the melted butter. Press the buttery crumbs into the base of the prepared cake pan firmly using the back of a spoon. Wrap the outside of the pan in cling film/plastic wrap and place in a roasting pan half full with water, ensuring that the water is not so high as to spill out. Set aside.

For the filling, whisk together the cream cheese, clotted cream, double/heavy cream, sugar, pumpkin purée, eggs, cinnamon, mixed/apple pie spice and vanilla bean paste in a blender or with an electric whisk. Pour the mixture over the crumb base and transfer the cheesecake, in its waterbath, to the preheated oven. Bake in the preheated oven for 45–60 minutes until the cheesecake is set but still wobbles slightly in the centre. Turn the oven off and leave the cheesecake in the oven until cool. Chill in the refrigerator for at least 3 hours, then dust the top with icing/confectioners' sugar and cinnamon to serve.

Tip: To prepare your own pumpkin purée, peel and chop pumpkin or butternut squash, then wrap in foil with a little water and a drizzle of maple syrup. Roast in a moderate oven until the flesh is soft, then purée in a food processor until smooth.

Greek baklava cheesecake

Baklava is one of my favourite sweet treats. It is not difficult to prepare and the end result is a delicious syrupy buttery pastry which is perfect with a mug of strong coffee. This is my version of baklava with a lemony cheesecake filling that really goes well with the crunch of the cinnamon nuts.

9 large sheets filo/phyllo pastry
(about 400 g/14 oz.)

120 g/1 stick butter, melted

3–4 tablespoons runny Greek honey

pistachios, for sprinkling

FOR THE CHEESECAKE FILLING

225 g/1 cup quark/farmer cheese

150 g/⅔ cup cream cheese

1 small egg, plus 1 egg yolk

50 g/¼ cup caster/white sugar

grated zest of 1 lemon

75 g/¾ cup ground almonds

FOR THE NUT FILLING

100 g/¾ cup pistachios

50 g/¼ cup caster/white sugar,
plus extra for sprinkling

2 teaspoons ground cinnamon

a piping bag fitted with a large round nozzle/tip

a 23-cm/9-inch round springform cake pan or tarte tatin pan, greased and lined

SERVES 10

Preheat the oven to 180°C (350°F) Gas 4.

To prepare the cheesecake filling, whisk together the quark/farmer cheese, cream cheese, egg and egg yolk, sugar, lemon zest and almonds in a large mixing bowl until the mixture is smooth and creamy. Spoon the mixture into the piping bag.

For the nut filling, blitz the pistachios with the sugar and cinnamon in a food processor until finely chopped.

Remove the filo/phyllo pastry from the packet and cut the sheets in half so that you are left with 18 smaller sheets. Cover with a damp tea towel/dish towel, which will prevent it from drying out and cracking. Lay one sheet of filo/phyllo on a clean work surface and brush with the melted butter using a pastry brush. Cover with a second sheet of filo/phyllo and brush with butter again. Sprinkle with a few tablespoons of the nut mixture so that the whole sheet is covered in a thin layer of nuts, then cover with a third sheet of filo/phyllo and brush again with butter. Pipe a line of the cheesecake filling along one of the long edges, then roll up so that the filling is in the middle of each tube.

Place the filo/phyllo tube around the edge of the prepared cake pan. Repeat with the remaining pastry until you have made 6 tubes of cheesecake pastry in total. Continue to arrange them in the pan in a spiral so that the ends of each tube touch, then brush the top of the pastry with a little more butter and bake in the preheated oven for 20–30 minutes until the top of the pastry is crisp and golden.

Heat the honey in a saucepan until it becomes thin and easily pourable then spoon over the baklava and leave to cool completely. Sprinkle with bright green pistachios and a little sugar, to serve.

cardamom bun cheesecake

At Easter in Sweden, *semlor* are served. There are a huge number of varieties and a very competitive edge between bakeries as to who can produce the best ones. *Semlor* are light dough buns, scented with cardamom and filled with ribbons of marzipan and whipped cream. This is my cheesecake version with a cheesecake filling on top of the dough. It is perfect served with an afternoon cup of tea or coffee.

FOR THE DOUGH

20 cardamom pods

200 ml/¾ cup warm milk

7 g/¼ oz. fast action yeast

30 g/2½ tablespoons granulated sugar

460 g/3½ cups plain/all-purpose flour, sifted, plus extra for dusting

½ teaspoon salt

2 eggs, beaten

60 g/4 tablespoons butter, softened

FOR THE FILLING

250 g/generous 1 cup mascarpone cheese

1 egg

50 g/¼ cup caster/white sugar

1 vanilla pod/bean

FOR THE TOPPING

250 ml/1 cup double/heavy cream

200 g/7 oz. marzipan (I use Anthon Berg)

icing/confectioners' sugar, for dusting

a 34 x 24-cm/13 x 9½-inch roasting pan, greased

a piping bag fitted with a large nozzle/tip

MAKES 12

For the dough, crush the cardamom pods in a pestle and mortar and remove the green husks. Grind the black seeds to a fine powder.

Place the warm milk, yeast and sugar in a jug/pitcher, whisk together and leave in a warm place for about 10 minutes until a thick foam has formed on top of the milk.

Meanwhile, sift the flour into a large mixing bowl, add the salt, eggs, butter and cardamom powder and mix together to incorporate, then pour in the yeast mixture. Using a stand mixer fitted with a dough hook, mix the dough on a slow speed for 2 minutes, then increase the speed and knead for about 8 minutes until the dough is very soft and pliable. Alternatively, knead the dough by hand for about 10–15 minutes.

For the cheesecake filling, whisk together the mascarpone, egg and sugar in a large mixing bowl until smooth. Cut the vanilla pod/bean in half and remove the seeds using the back of a knife, then stir them into the mixture.

With your hands, press the dough out to cover the bottom of the prepared pan, then spread the cheesecake mixture over the top of the dough, leaving a small gap around the edge. Place the pan in a warm place for about 1 hour or until the dough has doubled in size.

Preheat the oven to 180°C (350°F) Gas 4.

Bake the bun in the oven for 20–30 minutes until the dough is golden brown and sounds hollow when you tap it. Leave to cool, then slice into 12 squares with a sharp serrated knife.

Spoon the whipped cream into the piping bag and pipe stars of the cream on top of each cheesecake square. Using a swivel vegetable peeler or sharp knife, cut thin ribbons of the marzipan and scatter on top of the cream. (I find that chilling the marzipan in the freezer for about 10 minutes first makes it easier to cut.) Dust with icing/confectioners' sugar to serve.

As this contains fresh cream, it needs to be eaten straight away or stored in the refrigerator. This needs to be eaten on the day it is made.

Polish cheesecake

When I was writing this book, a friend told me that the best cheesecake they had ever eaten came from a Polish delicatessen in a nearby town. Not one to miss out on something yummy, I tracked down the cheesecake and it was of course delicious! This is my version. Twaróg cheese is a traditional Polish cheese, somewhat similar to cottage cheese. You need to pass it through a sieve/strainer before using otherwise the cheesecake will have a grainy texture. Twaróg cheese has a distinct sharp flavour with hints of lemon so I have not added any additional flavouring to this cheesecake, but you could add berries, lemon zest or vanilla if you wish. If you are short of time you could use 375 g/14 oz. readymade sweet shortcrust pastry. This is delicious served with poached fruits.

FOR THE PASTRY CRUST

120 g/1 stick butter, chilled

230 g/1¾ cups plain/all-purpose flour

50 g/¼ cup caster/white sugar

2 egg yolks

1 tablespoon cream cheese

a splash of milk, to glaze

FOR THE FILLING

500 g/generous 2 cups twaróg cheese

250 g/generous 1 cup cream cheese

4 eggs, separated

400 g/1¾ cups condensed milk

125 g/1 stick plus 1 tablespoon butter, melted

icing/confectioners' sugar, for dusting

a deep 30 x 22-cm/12 x 9-inch roasting pan, greased

leaf pastry cutters

SERVES 14

For the pastry crust, rub the butter into the flour until it resembles fine breadcrumbs. Add the sugar, egg yolks and cream cheese and mix together to a soft dough with your fingers, adding a little extra flour if the mixture is too sticky, or a little chilled water if it is too dry. Wrap the pastry dough in cling film/plastic wrap and chill in the refrigerator for 1 hour.

Bring the dough back to room temperature and, on a lightly floured surface, roll it out to a sheet large enough to line the roasting pan. Lay the pastry into the prepared pan and trim the edges. Roll out the trimmings and cut out small leaf shapes to decorate the cheesecake with.

Preheat the oven to 170°C (325°F) Gas 3.

To make the filling, pass the twaróg cheese through a fine mesh sieve/strainer. In a large mixing bowl, whisk the strained twaróg, cream cheese, eggs and condensed milk together until you have a smooth cream. Slowly pour in the melted butter, whisking all the time. Pour the mixture into the pastry case, arrange the pastry leaves on top. Brush the leaves with a little milk, to glaze, then bake in the preheated oven for 45–60 minutes until the cheesecake is golden brown and still wobbles slightly in the centre. Remove from the oven and leave to cool, then chill in the refrigerator before serving.

To serve, cut the chilled cheesecake into squares and dust with icing/confectioners' sugar. This is delicious served with poached fruits.

Japanese cherry blossom cheesecake

This cheesecake was inspired by my friend Justina who loves all things Japanese, particularly the cherry blossom season. The decoration is quick to prepare but looks so pretty and makes this a perfect springtime cheesecake.

FOR THE CAKE BASE

55 g/4 tablespoons butter, softened

55 g/¼ cup caster/white sugar

1 egg

2 teaspoons matcha powder

1 generous tablespoon crème fraîche

55 g/scant ½ cup self-raising flour, sifted

FOR THE FILLING

4 sheets leaf gelatine

200 g/scant 1 cup cream cheese

250 g/generous 1 cup ricotta

1 teaspoon vanilla bean paste

100 g/½ cup caster/white sugar

150 ml/⅔ cup double/heavy cream

400 g/1½–2 cups cherry compôte

FOR THE DECORATION

30 g/1 oz. dark chocolate, melted

sugar flowers

a 23-cm/9-inch round springform cake pan, greased and lined

a piping bag fitted with a small round nozzle/tip

SERVES 12

Preheat the oven to 180°C (350°F) Gas 4.

For the cake base, whisk together the butter and sugar in a large mixing bowl until creamy. Add the egg and beat again. Dissolve the matcha powder in 1 tablespoon hot water and add to the cake mixture along with the crème fraîche. Sift the flour over the mixture and fold in so that everything is incorporated. Pour the cake batter into the prepared baking pan and bake in the preheated oven for 15–20 minutes until the cake is golden brown and springs back when pressed gently in the centre. Leave to cool in the pan.

For the filling, soak the gelatine leaves in water until they are soft.

In a large mixing bowl, whisk the cream cheese, ricotta, vanilla and sugar together until light and creamy.

Put the cream in a heatproof bowl set over a pan of simmering water and heat gently. Squeeze the water out of the gelatine leaves and add them to the warm cream, stirring until dissolved. Pass the cream through a sieve/strainer to remove any undissolved gelatine pieces, then whisk into the cheese mixture.

Blitz the cherry compôte in a blender or food processor to make a smooth purée. Spread one third of the cherry purée over the cake base, leaving a small gap around the edge of the cake. Fold the remaining cherry purée into the cheesecake mixture, stopping before it is fully incorporated to make a pretty swirled pattern. Pour the cheesecake mixture over the base and smooth level, then leave to set in the refrigerator for 3 hours or overnight.

To decorate, spoon the melted chocolate into the piping bag and pipe delicate chocolate branches on top of the cheesecake. Fix sugar flowers to the branches using a little extra chocolate so that they look like cherry blossom branches.

whisky and raspberry cranachan cheesecakes

This cheesecake is inspired by the classic Scottish dessert, cranachan – whipped cream flavoured with whisky and honey folded through with toasted oats and fresh raspberries.

FOR THE FLAPJACK BASE

50 g/3½ tablespoons butter

30 g/2½ tablespoons caster/white sugar

40 g/2 tablespoons golden/light corn syrup

100 g/1 cup rolled oats

a pinch of salt

FOR THE FILLING

150 g/1–1¼ cups raspberries

80 ml/⅓ cup whisky

300 g/1⅓ cups cream cheese

300 ml/1¼ cups crème fraîche

80 ml/¼ cup honey

2 eggs

generous 1 tablespoon flour, sifted

TO SERVE

fresh raspberries

pouring cream

a baking sheet, greased

8 x 6-cm/2½-inch diameter chef's rings, greased and placed on a greased baking sheet

MAKES 8

Preheat the oven to 170°C (325°F) Gas 3.

For the flapjack base, heat the butter, sugar and golden/corn syrup together in a saucepan until the butter and sugar have melted and the mixture is syrupy. Stir in the oats and salt and mix well so that all the oats are coated.

Spoon the mixture onto the prepared baking sheet and flatten with the back of a spoon. Bake in the preheated oven for 20–30 minutes until the flapjack is golden brown. Remove from the oven and leave to cool for a few minutes. Whilst still warm, use one of the chef's rings to stamp out 8 rounds of flapjack to use as bases, then leave them to cool completely. Leave the oven on.

For the filling, soak the raspberries in the whisky for 30 minutes.

In a large mixing bowl, whisk together the cream cheese and crème fraîche. Whisk in the honey, eggs and flour, then fold through the raspberries and any remaining soaking whisky. Spoon the mixture into the chef's rings on the baking sheet and bake in the preheated oven for 25–30 minutes until golden brown on top. Leave to cool then transfer to the refrigerator to chill for at least 3 hours or preferably overnight.

When you are ready to serve, place a flapjack disc on each plate and top with a cheesecake. Serve with extra fresh raspberries and cream and a tot of whisky if you wish.

Black Forest cheesecake

FOR THE BASE

55 g/4 tablespoons butter

55 g/¼ cup caster/white sugar

1 egg

55 g/scant ½ cup self-raising flour

15 g/2½ teaspoons cocoa powder

1 generous tablespoon crème fraîche

2 tablespoons kirsch

270 g (drained weight)/2 cups morello cherries in syrup, plus 2 tablespoons of the syrup

FOR THE FILLING

300 g/1⅓ cups cream cheese

250 g/generous 1 cup ricotta

4 eggs

400 g/1¾ cups condensed milk

200 g/7 oz. dark chocolate, melted and cooled

FOR THE TOPPING

250 ml/1 cup double/heavy cream, whipped to stiff peaks

chocolate sprinkles

a 20-cm/8-inch square springform cake pan, greased and lined

a piping bag fitted with a star nozzle/tip

SERVES 12

This is my twist on the kitschy 1970s favourite German dessert – Black Forest gâteau. With a boozy cherry-soaked sponge base and rich chocolate cream filling, this is a perfect retro dinner party dessert. Serve with extra pouring cream if you want to be super indulgent!

Preheat the oven to 180°C (350°F) Gas 4.

For the base, whisk together the butter and sugar in a large mixing bowl until light and creamy. Beat in the egg and whisk again. Sift in the flour and the cocoa and fold through gently together with the crème fraîche. Spoon into the prepared cake pan and spread out evenly in a thin layer over the base. Bake in the preheated oven for 10–15 minutes until the sponge springs back when you press it with a clean finger. Allow the sponge base to cool in the pan, then drizzle the kirsch and cherry syrup over the base. Sprinkle three quarters of the cherries in a layer over the base.

Preheat the oven to 160°C (325°F) Gas 3.

For the filling, whisk together the cream cheese and ricotta in a large mixing bowl, until smooth and creamy. Add the eggs, condensed milk and cooled melted chocolate and whisk again. Spoon the mixture into the baking pan over the cherries and bake in the preheated oven for 1–1¼ hours until the cheesecake is set but still has a slight wobble in the centre. Leave to cool in the pan, then refrigerate until you are ready to serve.

To serve, spread half the cream over the top of the cheesecake and decorate with the reserved cherries and chocolate sprinkles. Spoon the remaining cream into the piping bag and pipe small stars of cream around the edge of the cheesecake. Serve immediately or store in the refrigerator until needed.

tiramisù cheesecake

Tiramisù – meaning 'pick me up' – is the all-time favourite Italian dessert. This is my cheesecake version, packed with all the required elements of coffee and chocolate and a light chocolate sponge layered through the cheesecake.

FOR THE CAKE

115 g/1 stick butter

115 g/generous ½ cup caster/white sugar

2 eggs

100 g/¾ cup self-raising flour

15 g/2½ teaspoons cocoa powder

FOR THE FILLING

500 ml/generous 2 cups crème fraîche

500 g/generous 2 cups mascarpone cheese

3 tablespoons icing/confectioners' sugar, or to taste

TO ASSEMBLE

80 ml/⅓ cup double espresso coffee*

100 ml/⅓ cup amaretto

50 g/2 oz. nougat chocolate (such as Toblerone), coarsely grated

cocoa powder, for dusting

a 23-cm/9-inch round springform cake pan, greased and lined

SERVES 10

*If you don't have an espresso machine, dissolve 1 tablespoon coffee granules in 80 ml/⅓ cup hot water, then leave to cool before using in the recipe.

Preheat the oven to 180°C (350°F) Gas 4.

For the cake, cream together the butter and sugar until light and creamy using a whisk or electric mixer. Add the eggs and beat again. Sift in the flour and cocoa and fold in. Spoon the mixture into the prepared cake pan and bake in the preheated oven for 10–15 minutes or until the cake springs back to your touch. Leave to cool completely.

For the filling, whisk together the crème fraîche and mascarpone. Sift the icing/confectioners' sugar over the mixture and fold through. Taste the mixture for sweetness and add a little further sugar if you wish.

Remove the cake from the pan and cut it in half horizontally with a sharp serrated knife. Place the bottom half of the cake back in the pan.

Mix together the coffee and amaretto. Spoon half the coffee mixture over the bottom cake, sprinkle over half the grated chocolate and dust liberally with cocoa. Spoon half of the filling mixture into the pan and spread out evenly using a spatula, then dust with more cocoa powder. Place the second cake half on top and spoon over the remaining coffee mixture, sprinkle with the remaining grated chocolate and dust with cocoa powder again. Spoon over the remaining filling mixture and spread level. Dust the top of the cheesecake with cocoa powder and chill in the refrigerator overnight for best results.

To remove from the pan, slide a round-bladed knife around the sides of the chilled cheesecake before removing the sides of the pan, and serve.

index

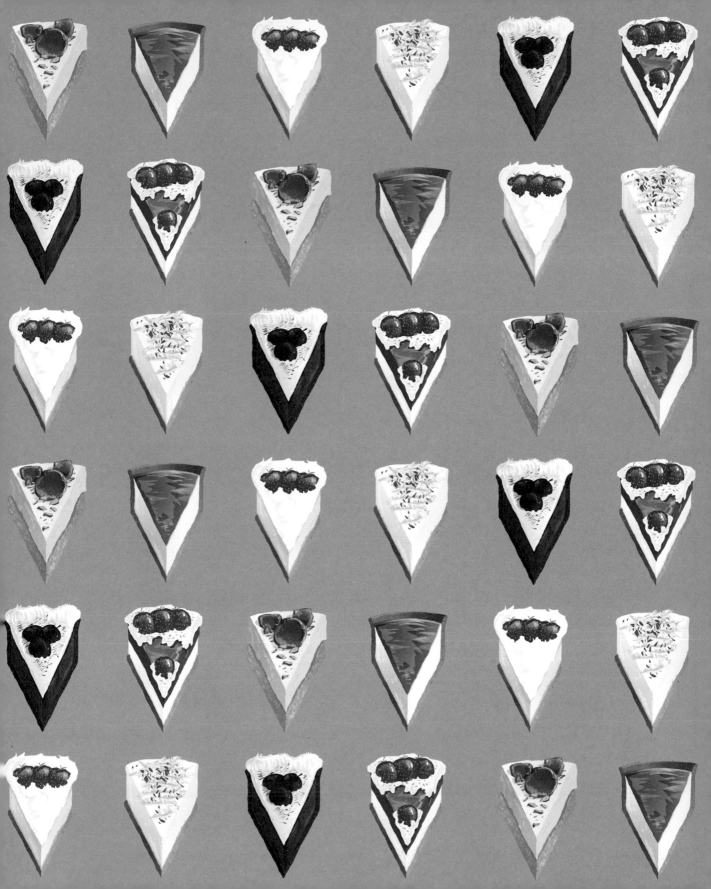

acknowledgments

With many thanks to all at RPS for allowing me to write this book – an utter delight despite the fact that it required consumption of 30 kilos of cream cheese! With particular thanks to Julia Charles for commissioning the book, Rebecca Woods for her patient editing and Lauren Wright for her fabulous PR support. To Steve Painter, Lucy McKelvie and Ellie Jarvis, my heartfelt thanks for the beautiful food styling and photography – how you managed to make 60 cheesecakes look so different is nothing short of miraculous! Particular thanks to Heather, Ellie and Claire of HHB agency for their continued support and to my family and friends who sampled and critiqued the cheesecakes – you went beyond the call of duty consuming so much cheesecake (particularly the Brown family of Stevington, who sampled 6 cheesecakes in one evening!) Thank you to the wonderful chefs Jon at the Emberton Bell and Bear and Chris at the Bildeston Crown for all the cheesecake discussions and inspiration. Finally special thanks to Gregg Wallace (lover of a good buttery biscuit base), for his kind endorsement of this book.